ACTS

Practical help and talk outlines
for Bible teachers and preachers
around the world

Written by
Graham Beynon

PPP thegoodbook COMPANY

PPP: Acts
© Graham Beynon/The Good Book Company, 2015.

Email: ppp@thegoodbook.co.uk

Published by
The Good Book Company
Tel (UK): 0333 123 0880
Tel (US): 866 244 2165
International: +44 (0) 208 942 0880
Email (UK): info@thegoodbook.co.uk
Email (US): info@thegoodbook.com

Websites:
UK: www.thegoodbook.co.uk
North America: www.thegoodbook.com
Australia: www.thegoodbook.com.au
New Zealand: www.thegoodbook.co.nz

ISBN: 9781784980061

Printed in India

The **Pray Prepare Preach** project is working in partnership with a growing number
of organisations worldwide, including: Langham Partnership • Grace Baptist Mission
• Pastor Training International (PTI) • Sovereign World Trust

Also in this series:

Teaching God's Big Story • Preaching Mark • Preaching Philippians • Preaching Job
• Teaching 2 Timothy • Teaching Deuteronomy • Teaching the Bible

Contents

PLEASE READ THIS FIRST!

It is a big joy to bring you another PPP book. We pray that this will help you to preach and teach God's word. We want people everywhere to hear God's word clearly. Then people will turn to Jesus. Christians will grow more like Jesus. God will have all the praise.

We give you a lot of help. But you must still work hard! Please do not just copy what you read!

PPP means Pray! Prepare! Preach! This book will help you to speak God's word if you are a preacher, or if you are a teacher of God's word in a school or church.

There is a lot to do before you preach or teach.

PRAY. We cannot change people's hearts. Only God can do that. We cannot make people believe. Only God can do that. We must pray before we prepare. Pray that you will hear God speak to you. We must pray before we speak. Pray that you will speak God's truth clearly. We must pray after we have taught God's word. Pray that your hearers respond to God's word.

PREPARE. It is hard work to prepare a Bible talk. It takes many hours. This book helps you, but it does not do all the work for you! You need to read the passage slowly. You need to study the verses carefully. You need to prepare what you will say to your hearers so that they will be helped.

PREACH. God works in wonderful ways when we teach his word! God's word is like seed that produces fruit in our lives—the fruit of the Spirit. It is exciting to speak God's word. God has promised that his word will do his work.

Here is the best way to use this book. Read the "How to teach and preach" section. Then begin at the start of Acts. Teach each section in turn. It is a story. It makes most sense when you begin at the start and end at the end!

"All Scripture is God-breathed and is useful for teaching, rebuking, correcting and training in righteousness, so that the servant of God may be thoroughly equipped for every good work" (2 Timothy 3:16-17).

QUICK HELP

How to prepare a talk on Acts

1. PRAY FOR GOD'S HELP

2. READ THE BIBLE SECTION SEVERAL TIMES

Use **Background** and **Understand** to help you study the Bible verses.

3. FIND THE MAIN POINT

Try to find the main point that God is teaching us in the Bible section. Use **Find the main point of the passage** to help you.

4. PLAN YOUR BIBLE TALK

Work out your sub-points, and how you will illustrate and apply your main point. Use the **PLAN** section to help you.

5. PREPARE

Prepare your talk to give it in your own language. Make notes to help you. Keep to the main point. Use our notes in the **TEACH** section to help you.

6. CHECK WHAT YOU HAVE DONE.

- Is the main point clear?
- Do you show them what the Bible teaches?
- Do you use word pictures to help your people understand and remember?
- Do you connect with the people?
- What do you hope will change?

7. PRAY

Pray that God will speak through your words and that his truth will change people.

For more help read the next section.

HOW TO USE THIS BOOK

Teaching the Bible is hard work. Paul tells Timothy: "Work hard so you can present yourself to God and receive his approval. Be a good worker, one who does not need to be ashamed and who correctly explains the word of truth" (2 Timothy 2:15).

- Why is it important to work hard at teaching the Bible?

Many teachers and preachers only spend a few minutes preparing a message. That is not enough. This is God's precious word. It needs hard work. It is like cooking and serving a good meal. It takes time and hard work to get ready. It must be balanced and tasty—good for everyone who listens. All must go away with food in their stomach which will help them to live for God.

- What will happen if we do not explain the Bible in the right way?

If we do not explain the Bible, God will be sad. Our people will not be helped. They will not grow strong.

If we *do* teach the Bible, people will be saved from hell. People will grow in the knowledge of Jesus and become more like Jesus.

STUDY, PLAN, TEACH

This book has divided the book of Acts into passages to preach or teach from. For each passage there are three parts to help you prepare: STUDY, PLAN, TEACH.

STUDY: How to understand the passage

You will see the following headings in the STUDY section:

Background —> Read —> Understand —> Find the main point of the passage

Background
This means:

- Where the passage is in the book of the Bible.
- Where the book is in the whole Bible story and in history.
- What other parts of the Bible help to explain this passage.

Read
Read the Bible passage two or three times. Read it slowly and carefully. It is

best to read out loud. Read it in a different translation if you have one. The third time read it with your eyes and ears, your nose and hands! Imagine you are there. What do you see, hear, smell and feel?

Understand

To teach a passage well you need to understand clearly what it says. Go through it verse by verse. Read each verse and then say what happens in your own words. This will help you to know what the passage is about.

There are questions in this book which will help you understand the passage, and notes to explain difficult words.

Find the main point of the passage

The main point is the big thing God says in each passage. It is important that you find this IN the passage. There are questions to help you.

PLAN: How to plan a sermon from the passage

The following headings are in the PLAN section:

Main point of the sermon —> Sub-points —> Illustrate —> Apply —> Review

Main point of the sermon

A sermon explains the passage, and it also applies the passage to the hearer. Look at the main point of the passage. Look for the things in the main point which are the same today. Remember that God does not change. People's hearts are the same. But remember we live after Jesus Christ and the cross. From the main point of the passage write the main point of your sermon, which applies for today.

Sub-points

- Sub-points explain a part of the MAIN POINT.
- Sub-points explain one part of the passage.
- Sub-points are short so your hearers can remember them.

There are sub-points suggested but you may want to use your own sub-points.

Illustrate

An illustration or word picture helps your hearers understand the main points you make. Sometimes there are illustrations in the passage. Sometimes you need to think of your own illustration. Make sure the illustration is easy to understand and connects with your people. It will help them remember and understand the main point of the sermon.

You may take a visual aid or picture. You may draw a picture or do a short drama. Always make sure it helps teach the main point!

Apply

When we teach God's word, we want God's word to speak to us and change all who hear it. So you must think how the main point of the passage applies to the people YOU speak to. Think of the different people you will speak to. How does the main point speak to older believers, new believers, and those who are not believers?

Review

Before you give your sermon or talk, you must review what you prepared.

- Check what you have prepared: Is the main point clear?
- Do you show what the Bible teaches in THAT passage?
- Have you thought of word pictures or illustrations to help people understand and remember the main point of the message?
- Do you have a clear flow to your talk so people can follow what you say?
- What do you want God to change in the lives of your hearers?

TEACH: How to give a sermon or talk from the passage

You will see the following headings in the TEACH section:

Start —> Explain —> Illustrate —> Apply —> End —> Pray

This section will help you write a sermon or talk on the Bible passage. It is not a complete sermon—you will need to do your own work as well. But it gives you ideas. You must take the ideas and use them in the best way for you and your people.

Always remember that the talk should be based on the main point.

Start

Think carefully about how to start your talk. It is good to tell your people the main point. Tell them why they need to listen and how this passage will help them. You can ask a question and tell them you will answer it in your talk. You need to get their interest so that they will listen.

Explain

This book gives you some ideas, but you will also need to add your own. Think of what is good for your people and what will help them to understand clearly. It is good to keep reading out the verses from the Bible as you explain them. Get your people to follow in their Bibles. Make sure your hearers can see that what you say is what the Bible says!

Illustrate

In the PLAN section there is one main illustration. You may need to think of others also. Make sure these help people to remember and understand the main point of the sermon.

Apply

In the PLAN section you will have thought about how to apply the passage. It is important to make this as clear as possible. Give your hearers something to think about, or something to do. Remember that we want people to change and grow. Make sure you also say something to those who are not believers.

End

Think about how to end your talk. Remind your hearers of the main point. Help them to remember what it is.

Sometimes it is helpful to give your hearers time to think and pray about what they have heard before you carry on with the meeting.

Pray

Pray, and keep praying, both before and after you have given your talk.

- Pray God will first change you.
- Pray God will use your words to speak to your people.
- Pray God's truth will change your people.

INTRODUCTION TO ACTS

1. What the book of Acts is about

The book of Acts tells us about the first years after Jesus ascended back to heaven. We are told how Jesus' followers received the Holy Spirit and gathered together as God's people, and how they spread the message about Jesus.

The main topics we learn about are:

- how God's people lived.
- how the message about Jesus spread.
- how new groups of people joined the church.
- how God's promises came true.
- opposition to and persecution of God's people and the message about Jesus.

Acts was written by Luke, who also wrote the Gospel of Luke. Luke wrote his story about the life of Jesus, and then wrote the book of Acts to continue the story. We see this in the first verses of Acts:

> "In my former book, Theophilus, I wrote about all that Jesus began to do and to teach until the day he was taken up to heaven, after giving instructions through the Holy Spirit to the apostles he had chosen."
>
> (Acts 1:1-2)

The book of Acts then explains what Jesus continued to do by his Spirit, and through his followers.

At the end of Luke's Gospel we are told Jesus is the risen Saviour. God's plans to rescue sinners reach their highest point in Jesus. In Acts we see how God's plan to save sinners by faith in Jesus continued and reached out to all nations.

The book's full title is: "The Acts of the Apostles". Sometimes people say it should be called: "The Acts of the Holy Spirit". It might be best to call it: "The Acts of the Risen Lord Jesus"—Jesus worked through his people, who were given power by the Holy Spirit.

2. Why Luke wrote the book of Acts

Luke tells us his purpose in writing at the start of Luke's Gospel, the first part of his story of Jesus' life:

> "Many have undertaken to draw up an account of the things that have been fulfilled among us, just as they were handed down to us by those who from the first were eyewitnesses and servants of the word. With this in mind, since I myself have carefully investigated everything from the beginning, I too decided to write an orderly account for you, most excellent Theophilus, so that you may know the certainty of the things you have been taught."
>
> (Luke 1:1-4)

Luke wrote for someone who knew about Jesus and what Jesus had done. Theophilus was a believer in Jesus already. Luke wanted him to be certain of the truth about Jesus. Luke wrote his Gospel, and then Acts, so that people would grow stronger in their faith.

In the book of Acts Luke tells how **God was fulfilling his plan of salvation—God's plan to bring sinners to know him and follow him**. Luke shows how the events in Acts fit with the Old Testament. This shows clearly that it is true.

In Acts, Luke also **gives answers to specific questions** the church faced. These were questions which may have caused them to doubt:

- Why are Christians persecuted?
- How are new people included in the church?
- Do Gentiles (people who are not Jews) have to obey the Old Testament law?
- Is Paul a true apostle?

In answering these questions Luke wanted to strengthen people's confidence.

Luke explains the spread of the good news about Jesus so that **believers would be certain that it is God's message**. God's people were persecuted for spreading the message. But that should not cause them to doubt. The gospel is God's message of salvation. It shows how the risen Lord Jesus rescues sinners. People could be confident that God would make sure this message keeps on spreading.

So as we preach the book of Acts, we want people to grow in confidence in the message about Jesus and how to live for him. We want them to know for certain this is the way God works in the world: this is how God keeps all his promises. And so we want people to grow in certainty about their faith in God.

Remember how Acts fits into the big story of the Bible.

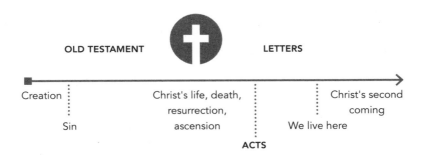

3. Acts is a history book

The Bible has different kinds of writings. There is history (for example Genesis, Exodus, 1 Samuel, Acts), songs (Psalms), wisdom literature (Proverbs), prophecy (for example, Isaiah, Malachi), Gospels (for example, Matthew, Mark), and letters (for example, Romans, Jude). When we teach the Bible we must know which kind of writing we are teaching. Preaching Proverbs is very different to preaching Romans because it is a different kind of writing.

Acts is a narrative which tells the history of the spread of the good news after the resurrection and ascension of Jesus.

OVERVIEW OF ACTS

Luke divides Acts into clear sections.

There is a **division by geography**. Acts 1:8 says that followers of Jesus will be his witnesses in three areas: Jerusalem, Samaria and Judea, and the ends of the earth. This structure is then followed in the book:

- Chapters 1 – 7 are based in Jerusalem.
- Chapters 8 – 12 are based in Judea and Samaria.
- Chapters 13 – 28 are about the gospel spreading in the Roman Empire.

Luke divides these sections into smaller sections. He does this by **using a repeated phrase**.

These are the similar phrases:

Acts 6:7	"So the word of God spread. The number of disciples in Jerusalem increased rapidly, and a large number of priests became obedient to the faith."
Acts 9:31	"Then the church throughout Judea, Galilee and Samaria enjoyed a time of peace and was strengthened. Living in the fear of the Lord and encouraged by the Holy Spirit, it increased in numbers."
Acts 12:24	"But the word of God continued to spread and flourish."
Acts 16:5	"So the churches were strengthened in the faith and grew daily in numbers."
Acts 19:20	"In this way the word of the Lord spread widely and grew in power."

Each of these comes at an important point in the story. The theme in each section is a bit different. Here is an outline:

Section One (1:1 – 6:7)
The Holy Spirit arrives and fulfils the Old Testament promise. The good news spreads in Jerusalem among Jews. There is some opposition but not very much. The focus is on the actions of the apostles led by Peter.

Section Two (6:8 – 9:31)
The good news about Jesus spreads outside Jerusalem, especially in Samaria. People who are not Jews respond to the good news and receive the Holy Spirit. They are Samaritans, who are related to the Jews. There is a rise in opposition and persecution. The focus in this section is on new people, not on the apostles.

Section Three (9:32 – 12:24)

The good news spreads to Gentiles (non-Jews), who also receive the Holy Spirit. The focus is on Peter again. We also see the relationship between Jewish and Gentile Christians in Antioch.

Section Four (12:25 – 16:5)

The good news spreads into new areas. The first missionary journey starts with Paul and Barnabas travelling from Antioch. This raises questions about how non-Jews will be included in the church and if they need to obey the Old Testament law. This question is settled at a meeting in Jerusalem. The focus is on Paul and Barnabas.

Section Five (16:6 – 19:19)

This is Paul's second and third missionary journey. The focus is on Paul and how he takes the good news to Gentiles. There is a lot of opposition from Jews.

Section Six (19:19 – 28:31)

The focus is on Paul and his journey to Jerusalem and then to Rome. We are told about his trial in front of official leaders. There is much about defending the truth of the message about Jesus. We see how God protects Paul so that the message about Jesus will keep on spreading.

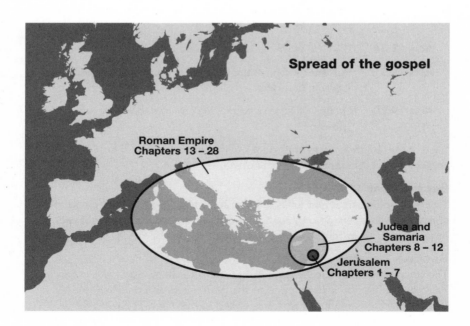

Spread of the gospel

Roman Empire
Chapters 13 – 28

Judea and
Samaria
Chapters 8 – 12

Jerusalem
Chapters 1 – 7

⬆ STUDY
THE NEW JOB

Background

READ Luke 1:1-4

- Why did Luke write the Gospel of Luke and the book of Acts?

READ Luke 24:36-53 and Acts 1:1-2

- What is Jesus' job for his apostles?
- What will the book of Acts be about?

Note: The apostles are the twelve men Jesus chose to be his special representatives (Luke 6:12-16).

Read

READ Acts 1:1-11 two or three times.

Read it in a different translation if you have one. Go through verse by verse, explaining to yourself in your own words what happens.

Understand

READ Acts 1:3 again.

- Why do you think it was so important for the apostles to know that Jesus truly was alive?
- What did Jesus teach his apostles about?

Jesus gives "many convincing proofs" so that the apostles know he is truly alive. This means they know that Jesus is God's King or Messiah.

Jesus teaches his apostles about the "kingdom of God". That is God's rule over his world. In the Old Testament God promised he would rule the world one day. This has started through Jesus. That is why Jesus said he brought the kingdom of God (Luke 4:43). God's kingdom is now over those who believe in Jesus and bow to him.

READ Acts 28:30-31

The book of Acts starts and ends with teaching about the kingdom of God. The book tells how God's kingdom grows. It tells how people come to have God as the King of their lives. The kingdom spreads through Jesus' followers telling people that Jesus is God's risen King.

READ Acts 1:4-5 again.

- What is the gift the Father promised?
- Why do you think Jesus mentions John the Baptist?

In the Old Testament God promised he will work in a new way by his Spirit. See Jeremiah 31:31-34, Ezekiel 36:24-27. These passages show that God will give people his Holy Spirit. The Holy Spirit works in people so that they obey God.

John the Baptist said this (see Luke 3:15-17). John said that Jesus, who comes after him, will bring the Holy Spirit.

READ Acts 1:6-8 again.

- What do the apostles ask about restoring the kingdom?
- What is Jesus' reply?

The apostles ask if all of God's promises are about to come true. Jesus says they cannot know when the final restoring will happen. But they have a new job to do. They must be his witnesses. This means they must tell people what they have seen and that Jesus is God's risen King.

Acts shows how the apostles tell people in Jerusalem, Judea and Samaria, and to the ends of the earth. God's message about Jesus must spread to all nations (see Isaiah 49:6).

The apostles were in a different situation to us. They were witnesses to Jesus' resurrection. We are not witnesses in the same way as them. But we can point people to the witness of the apostles in the Bible—it is a record of what they saw.

READ Acts 1:9-11 again.

- What do the angels tell the disciples?

The word "heaven" or "sky" is repeated here (it is the same word). Jesus is taken into heaven. His disciples must focus on life on earth and remember that Jesus will come back from heaven as King.

Find the main point of the passage

- What is the main thing Luke says?
- What new job do the disciples have?

Jesus is alive and so he is God's King and Saviour. God is working in a new way through Jesus. His followers must now be witnesses to him: They must tell others what they have seen. Everyone must hear about Jesus.

So the main point is that God's kingdom has come through Jesus the risen King. His followers must tell everyone about Jesus before he returns.

 PLAN

Main point of the sermon

A sermon explains the passage, and applies the passage to the hearers. Look at the main point of the passage. Write out what this main point will mean for your hearers.

It will be something like this: Jesus is the risen King who will rule for God. His followers are to tell people about him.

Sub-points

What breaks are there in the passage? What is the point of each section?

Verses 1-3
Introduction to the book and what Jesus does as God's risen King.

Verses 4-5
Jesus promises his followers the gift of the Holy Spirit.

Verses 6-11
Jesus teaches his apostles that they will be given power by the Holy Spirit to speak the good news.

Think of a heading for each sub-point.

For example:

1. Jesus is God's risen King (v1-3)
2. Jesus promises the Holy Spirit (v4-5)
3. So God's people have a new job (v6-11)

Check that your sub-points come from the main point of the passage.

Illustrate

The main point is about the new work the apostles have. This is because of the new situation: Jesus is God's risen King, who has left them and gone to heaven.

Think of a new situation that results in new work. For example: If you are given a new job, you have new responsibilities. Or if you become a mother, you have new work to do to feed your baby and look after him or her.

Apply

- What reassures and encourages Christians from this passage?

We can know that God's plan to rescue sinners was fulfilled in Jesus. God's message of salvation is now spreading across the world. This will continue until Jesus returns. We know the Holy Spirit will help us in this task.

Review

Check the main point is clear and that you keep to THIS passage.

 # TEACH

Start

Give your illustration of a new situation which results in new work to do.

We can find it hard to tell people about Jesus. We may not feel people need to hear. We may feel afraid. We may feel weak. The government may not allow us.

Talk about some of the barriers to speaking about Jesus in your place.

Explain

Use your sub-points to explain the message. Get people to look at the Bible verses.

Jesus is God's risen King (v1-3)

This is after Jesus' death and resurrection, but before he returns to heaven. Jesus proves to his disciples that he is alive so that they know he is God's risen King. His death was part of God's plan to rescue sinners. Jesus teaches them about God's kingdom. The whole book of Acts is about that kingdom—*read Acts 28:31.*

Jesus promises the Holy Spirit (v4-5)

Jesus says that God's promise of the Holy Spirit will now come true. This means that the time God promised has arrived.

Explain some of the Old Testament passages that look forward to the coming of the Holy Spirit.

So God's people have a new job (v6-11)

The apostles must get on with the new job of being God's witnesses. They must tell people what God has done through Jesus. The Holy Spirit will give them strength to do this. We will see the spread of this message in the book of Acts. God's people must carry on this work until Jesus returns.

Apply

Remind your hearers of the difficulties in telling others about Jesus that you talked about at the start. How does this passage answer those problems? What new work do we have? Why must we get on with it?

End

Jesus is God's risen King, so we must tell people about him. Remember that we have the Holy Spirit to strengthen us to be his witnesses.

Pray

Pray that God will encourage you and your hearers to know that Jesus rules in heaven. Pray you will know the power of the Holy Spirit to be his witnesses.

⬆ STUDY
ACCORDING TO PLAN

Background

- Jesus has been raised from the dead, but what questions may his followers still have about his betrayal and death?
- Jesus was betrayed by one of his own disciples. How may that make them feel?

Jesus has ascended to heaven. He told his apostles to wait for the gift of the Holy Spirit. This passage is what happens while they wait.

Read

READ Acts 1:12-26 two or three times.

Explain each verse in your own words.

Understand

READ Acts 1:12-14

Verse 16: "Fulfilled" – a prediction that comes true.

- What does the list of apostles in verse 13 remind people about?

The believers are praying and waiting for the gift of the Holy Spirit. This reminds us that there are only eleven apostles. The missing one betrayed Jesus.

READ Acts 1:15-17

- How does Peter talk about Judas and his betrayal?

Peter does not hide how bad Judas' betrayal was. He makes it clear that Judas was one of the group of apostles. Judas was responsible for Jesus being arrested. But Peter says that Judas' betrayal had to happen. It fulfilled God's word in the Old Testament.

READ Acts 1:18-19

- What happened to Judas as a result of his betrayal?
- Who knew about this?

Peter says Judas got a reward of money. But his final reward was death. Everyone in Jerusalem knew what happened.

READ Acts 1:20 and look up the verses Peter mentions (Psalm 69:25, Psalm 109:8).

- Why does Peter quote these psalms?
- Why does Peter say they are about Jesus?

These psalms are about David and how David was betrayed. God organised for David's life to be a picture of what would happen to Jesus. So lots of things are the same for David and Jesus. Things that happened to David also happened to Jesus. This is why Peter says these verses are also about Judas and his betrayal of Jesus. David was opposed by an enemy whose "place was deserted", and so was Jesus. Someone else replaced David's enemy. So someone else must replace Jesus' enemy too.

READ Acts 1:21-22

- What does Peter think they must now do?
- What qualifications does this person need?

This Scripture shows they must choose another apostle. This must be someone who has seen all of Jesus' ministry. They must be a witness of Jesus' resurrection. This is because the apostles have the special role of being witnesses to Jesus.

READ Acts 1:23-26

- How do they decide who to choose?
- How do they fulfil what God said would happen?

It is Jesus who chooses the 12 apostles (We often refer to the 12 disciples, but we should really call them apostles. "Disciples" is a more general word for any follower of Jesus.) It is Jesus who chooses who will take the place of Judas. This is not a usual way to make a decision. It is because there were two suitable people and they believe Jesus must choose.

Find the main point of the passage

- What is the main thing these verses say?

These verses say that Judas' betrayal was part of God's plan. Choosing another apostle is also part of God's plan, which the apostles must carry out.

- What can we be sure of because of this passage?

We can be sure of God's sovereign plan—his plan for all time and over all things. We can be sure that nothing can catch God by surprise. We must be confident. We can be very sure that all God's plans will come true.

So the main point of the passage is that all of God's plan will be fulfilled.

 **PLAN**

Main point of the sermon

A sermon explains the passage, and applies the passage to the hearers. Look at the main point of the passage. Write out what this main point will mean for your hearers.

This passage is about how God's plans were fulfilled in an unexpected way.

The main point will be something like this: God's plans can never be stopped, so we should trust him.

Sub-points

What breaks are there in the passage? What are the points of the sections?

Verses 12-19
The believers remembered that Judas is not with them now. The Scripture in Psalms about Judas had to be fulfilled.

Verses 20-26
Psalm 69:25 was fulfilled in the death of Judas. Psalm 109:8 needs to be fulfilled, so the believers have to choose another apostle.

You may want to use these main themes:

1. God's plans were told before they happen (v12-17, 20)

2. God's plans are fulfilled (v18-19, 21-26)

Illustrate

The main point is about God being in control of everything that happens. Think of a situation that looked as if it was out of control, but actually someone was in charge. Imagine a thief plans to break in and enter. But he does not know the police are watching all that he does as part of their bigger plan.

Apply

- How does this passage encourage and comfort Christians?

We can be sure that Jesus did not make a mistake in choosing Judas. We can know that God is in control.

Give an example from your life or village of a time when things looked out of control—but behind it all God was working out his good plans.

- What confidence does this give us in reading the Bible?

We know that every time God says something will happen, it will definitely happen. So we can trust what God says.

Review

Check the main point is clear and that you keep to THIS passage.

 # TEACH

Start

Explain how people feel when surprising things happen, and it looks as if no one is in control. Give examples like losing a job, or a war.

Why did Judas betray Jesus? Did this mean Jesus made a mistake? Did God know what was going to happen?

Talk about how we feel when we think God is not in control. We are not sure if we can really trust God.

Explain

Use your sub-points to explain the verses. Get people to look at the Bible verses.

God's plans were told before they happen (v12-17, 20)

Answer the questions about Judas above. Look at verse 16: "Scripture had to be fulfilled". Peter says everything went according to God's plan. Everyone was surprised by Judas. But God foretold this in the Old Testament. The psalms about David give a picture of what would happen to Jesus. There are similar things in David's life and Jesus' life. So someone must take the place of Judas.

God's plans are fulfilled (v18-19, 21-26)

What God said has come true. Judas' place has been "deserted" (become empty). What happened to

Judas is a reminder of what happens to those who go against or oppose God.

God said that Judas would be replaced. So the apostles must now choose another apostle. They choose between two men by casting lots. This is how Jesus shows who he wants. This is not a way to make decisions today (we never see it done again in the Bible).

Use your illustration. It looked as if God was not in control. But all went exactly according to God's plan.

Apply

Talk about the difference it makes to know God is in control. This gives us confidence in God. We can be completely certain of God's plans to rescue sinners. Nothing will ever surprise God. God's plans will always come true. We can be sure of this even when things surprise us.

End

God is in control. His plans will always come true. We can be confident of God.

Pray

Pray you will be confident of God and amazed at his control over everything. Pray this truth will make you sure and certain.

3 ⬆ STUDY
THE PROMISE ARRIVES

Background

Jesus has ascended to heaven. His followers have chosen another apostle to take the place of Judas. They are waiting for the gift of the Holy Spirit. This passage tells how the Holy Spirit arrived and Peter explained what happened.

Read

READ Acts 2:1-21 two or three times.

Explain each verse in your own words.

Understand

READ Acts 2:1-13

Verse 1: "Pentecost" – a Jewish festival fifty days after the Passover.

Verse 4: "Other tongues" – other languages.

- What is the result of the Holy Spirit filling people?
- How do the crowd in Jerusalem respond?
- Why does Luke tell us where people came from (v9-11)?

In the Old Testament wind and fire are a sign of God or his Holy Spirit. So this is a picture of God coming to his people. This group speak in different languages so that people from different countries hear their own language. Notice how Luke repeats this point (verses 6, 8, 11). God has fulfilled his promise to gather all his people to him again.

(This is a miracle of speech which is not the same as the "tongues" in 1 Corinthians 12 and 14.)

READ Ezekiel 36:24-32

- What did God promise he would do?
- How is this fulfilled in Acts 2?

God promised to gather his people together and give them his Spirit. This is what happens at Pentecost.

READ Acts 2:14-21

- What does Peter say is happening?
- What does verse 21 mean people can now do?

God is keeping his promise to give his Holy Spirit to everyone who believes. In the Old Testament God only gave the Holy Spirit to some people, like kings or prophets. Now God will give his Holy Spirit to all his people. This gift of God's Spirit is joined with God's offer to forgive sin. People can now call on the Lord and they will be saved (verse 21).

Prophecy, dreams and visions were signs of the Spirit's work in the Old Testament. Verse 17 is saying that everyone will know the work of God's Spirit.

Pentecost is a very significant moment. The gift of God's Spirit is to change people so they will follow God (see Ezekiel 36:27). God worked through Jesus' death and resurrection to keep that promise. This means that the "last days" have arrived (v17). They will continue until the "day of the Lord" (v20), when God will judge and re-create the world.

We will see more in the next passage about how people are saved. Here Peter just says we should "call on the name of the Lord".

Some people may have a question:

- Do we have to speak in tongues to receive God's Spirit?

No, we do not. Later, in verse 41, people are baptised but do not speak in tongues. Lots of people in Acts believe in Jesus without speaking in tongues. We will return to this question later in Acts.

Find the main point of the passage

- What is the main lesson from these verses?
- How should we feel because of this passage?

God's plan to rescue sinners was fulfilled by Jesus' death and resurrection. Through Jesus the gift of the Holy Spirit was given. We can call on God to save us. We do that by trusting in Jesus. Then we are saved from God's anger, we become one of God's people, and we receive God's Spirit. The Holy Spirit works in us so that we know God and will live for God.

So the main point of the passage is: God's promise to send his Holy Spirit has come true.

# ⬇ PLAN

Main point of the sermon

What will your sermon try to convince people of? What do they need to know about the Holy Spirit from this passage? What difference will that make?

The main point will be something like this: God kept his promises to bring salvation and give the gift of his Holy Spirit.

Sub-points

- Read the main point again.
- Read the verses again.
- What sub-points will help you teach this passage?

Verses 1-13

This part tells what happens. The Holy Spirit comes. People can speak in different languages. Jews from every nation are amazed.

Verses 14-21

Peter explains what has happened. God's promise in Joel 2 is fulfilled and so his Holy Spirit has come. People can call on God and be saved. If they do, then they will receive the Holy Spirit too.

Think of a heading for each sub-point.

For example:

1. The Holy Spirit comes (v1-13)

2. We can be saved and receive the Holy Spirit (v 14-21)

Illustrate

Use the illustration of making promises. For example, promising your children a special present or a holiday. One day the promise arrives—it's a wonderful day. God has kept his promise and a wonderful day has arrived for us.

Apply

- If you are not a true believer, what should you now do?

You should repent and trust in Jesus for forgiveness.

- If you are a believer, how should you feel about God's promise?

We should rejoice that God's promise of forgiveness is true. We should be glad we have the Holy Spirit in us.

- What will you say to someone who is not sure if they have the Holy Spirit?

As soon as someone trusts in Jesus to forgive them, then God gives them his Spirit as well.

Review

Check the main point is clear and that you keep to THIS passage.

 # TEACH

Start

Start with your illustration about a promise being made and waiting for it to come.

God made wonderful promises to save people and give his Spirit. This is the day when God kept that promise.

Explain

Use your sub-points to explain the message of these verses. Get people to look at the Bible verses.

The Holy Spirit comes (v1-13)

Remind people about Jesus' promise in 1:4-5. Explain what the wind and fire show. This is God arriving and living in his people in a new way. *Explain the miracle of speech.* Everyone can understand in their own language. Everyone is amazed and wonders what happened.

Point out that there are Jews from "every nation under heaven" (v5, 9-10). God promised to gather his people from all the nations where they were scattered in exile. When he did, he would give them his Spirit (Ezekiel 36:24-27).

We can be saved and receive the Holy Spirit (v14-21)

Peter says this is what Joel spoke about. *Explain God promised there* would be a time when the Holy Spirit would work in a new way. God's Spirit comes so we can know God ourselves, and he can work in us so we obey him.

Everyone who calls on God will be forgiven and receive the Holy Spirit. Everyone who truly believes in Jesus receives the Holy Spirit (v38).

Apply

God has kept his promise to forgive sinners and send his Holy Spirit. If we are not true believers, we must repent and trust in Jesus. Then we will be forgiven and receive God's Spirit ourselves. If we are believers, then we will rejoice! We will thank him for rescuing us from sin and for the Holy Spirit in our lives. We can be sure that if we have repented and believe in Jesus, we have the Holy Spirit and God is at work in us.

End

God has kept his promises. The day of salvation has arrived and the gift of the Holy Spirit is available.

Pray

Pray that you will rejoice in what God has done through Jesus. Thank God for his wonderful gifts of forgiveness and the Holy Spirit.

4 ⬆ STUDY
IT'S ALL ABOUT JESUS

Background

The Holy Spirit has arrived. Peter explained that God has kept his promise to bring forgiveness and the gift of his Holy Spirit. We stopped halfway through Peter's explanation. This passage looks at the rest of what he said. Peter explains how the arrival of the Holy Spirit connects to Jesus.

Read

READ Acts 2:22-41 two or three times.

Explain each verse in your own words.

Understand

READ verses 22-36

Verse 22: "Accredited" – shown to have authority.

Verse 31, 36: "Messiah" or "Christ" – God's anointed Saviour.

Verse 33: "Exalted" – lifted up to a position of authority.

Verse 37: "Cut to the heart" – very upset.

- What does Peter say about Jesus in verses 22-24?
- How did Jesus fulfil what David said about him in Psalm 16:8-11 (see v25-31)?
- How are Jesus and the gift of the Holy Spirit connected (v32-33)?
- What is the conclusion about Jesus (v34-36)?

Peter summarises Jesus' life, death and resurrection. Peter says that killing Jesus was wicked or evil, but it was part of God's plan. Jesus now fulfils what David said. David knew God promised that one of David's descendants would rule for ever. But he himself died and stayed dead! So in Psalm 16 he was looking into the future as a prophet. He spoke about Jesus' resurrection.

Because Jesus was raised from death and went back to heaven, the Holy Spirit was given. Through Jesus, God's promises are fulfilled. This is proof that Jesus is God's exalted King (Lord) and Saviour (Messiah or Christ). Verse 36 is the conclusion to all Peter says. Notice the conclusion is about Jesus, not the Holy Spirit.

READ verses 37-41

Verse 38: "Repent" – to change direction, turn around.

- How do people respond to Peter?

- What does Peter tell them to do?
- What does Peter promise them?

People realise their sin and ask what they should do. Peter tells them to turn back to God (repent) and show their faith in Jesus (be baptised). Everyone who does this will be forgiven and will receive the Holy Spirit. Notice that when you repent and believe you immediately receive the Holy Spirit. It does not happen at a later point.

Find the main point of the passage

- What is the main lesson from these verses?
- What should we do because of this passage?

God's plans of salvation were fulfilled through Jesus' death and resurrection. Through Jesus the gift of the Holy Spirit was given. God has made Jesus "Lord" and "Messiah". Everyone should now turn back to God and believe in Jesus. And they need to show their faith in Jesus. They will be forgiven and receive the Holy Spirit. Notice that people need to respond to what God has done in Jesus—Jesus is the focus.

So the main point of the passage is: God has made Jesus Lord and Saviour. Everyone must repent, be forgiven and receive the Holy Spirit.

PLAN

Main point of the sermon

A sermon explains the passage, and applies the passage to the hearers. Look at the main point of the passage. Write what this main point will mean for your hearers.

Your main point will be something like this: Jesus is God's King and Saviour, and so we can be forgiven and receive the Holy Spirit.

Sub-points

- Read the main point again.
- Read the verses again.
- What sub-points will help you teach this passage?

Verses 22-36
Jesus' death was part of God's plan. God raised Jesus from the dead. Jesus is exalted as God's King and Saviour. As God's Saviour Jesus now gives the Holy Spirit.

Verses 37-41
The people realise killing Jesus was wrong. Peter tells them to repent and be baptised (v38). They will be forgiven and receive the Holy Spirit.

Think of headings for the sub-points.

1. Jesus is God's King and Saviour (v22-36)

2. So turn back to God (v37-41)

3. Be forgiven and receive the Holy Spirit (v37-41)

Illustrate

The main point is about who Jesus is: He is King and Saviour. That tells us how we should respond to Jesus and what we will receive from him. If someone is very important (for example, a king), it will change how you respond to them. It also changes what they can give you.

Apply

- What does this passage tell us about Jesus?

He is God's King and Saviour. He has brought God's plans for forgiveness.

- What should someone who is not a believer do?

They should turn back to God and trust in Jesus.

- How does this passage help a believer to be sure about God's forgiveness?

It tells us that if we see who Jesus is and trust in him, God forgives us and gives us the Holy Spirit. How should a Christian feel about Jesus? We should be excited about what God has done through Jesus. We will respect Jesus and be so thankful for him.

Review

Check the main point is clear and that you keep to THIS passage.

 # TEACH

Start

This passage is about Jesus' identity, and what God has done through Jesus. We learn how we should respond to Jesus. If we respond to Jesus rightly, then God will give us the Holy Spirit.

You may start with your illustration about the importance of knowing who someone is (their identity). Or you may begin with different ideas people have about Jesus.

Explain

Jesus is God's King and Saviour (v22-36)

Peter is explaining why the Holy Spirit has come. It is because of what God has done through Jesus.

Explain the verses about Jesus' death and resurrection.

People killed Jesus because they did not accept who he is—the Messiah. But God raised Jesus from the dead. God fulfilled his promise to David. Jesus is exalted as God's King and Saviour. That is why the Holy Spirit has come.

So turn back to God (v37-41)

Explain the people's response.

They realise how wrong they were, and ask what to do. They must turn to God: We must too. We must trust in what God did in Jesus. We must show our belief by being baptised.

Be forgiven and receive the Holy Spirit (v37-41)

When we turn to God and trust him, we can be sure he will forgive our sin. And we will also receive the gift of God's Spirit. We can be sure that God has truly forgiven us, and that God is at work in us.

Apply

We must understand who Jesus is and what God has done through him. If we have not turned back to God, we must repent and be baptised. If we have done that already, we will rejoice in our forgiveness. We should also be sure that we have the Holy Spirit living in us. We can be thankful and celebrate how good God is to us.

End

Jesus is the King and the one who can save us from our sins. We can be forgiven and receive the Holy Spirit.

Pray

Pray you will clearly see who Jesus is. Pray you will rejoice in what God has done through Jesus. Thank Jesus for his two wonderful gifts— forgiveness and the Holy Spirit.

↑ STUDY
NEW COMMUNITY

Background

The Holy Spirit has come! Peter calls people to turn from their sins to Jesus and be baptised. Many see their sin and turn to God for forgiveness. They form a new group. They are the first church—people who trust in Jesus. Here are people who have repented, are forgiven, and are filled with the Holy Spirit. Now Luke explains how they live.

Read

READ Acts 2:42-47 two or three times.

Explain each verse in your own words.

Understand

READ Acts 2:42-43

Verse 42: "Devoted" – made a priority.

Verse 42: "Breaking of bread" – eating together; remembering Jesus' death.

- What do these new believers devote themselves to (spend all their time doing)?
- Why are these things so important?
- How does everyone feel?

Verse 42 gives their priorities. These are the things the new believers were "devoted" to. They spent their time and put their focus on these things.

- Apostles' teaching: This was the teaching from the apostles about Jesus.
- Fellowship: This was the shared life the Christians had together. "Fellowship" means what we share together.
- Breaking of bread: This refers to meals together. It was also a time to celebrate the Lord's Supper and remember Jesus' death (Luke 22:14-20).
- Prayer: Speaking to God. This probably included prayers of confession, thanksgiving, praise and requests.

Verse 43 says that everyone was filled with "awe"—this means respect, reverence, fear. God was working and this was an amazing time. They saw God's presence by miracle signs from the apostles.

READ verses 44-47

- How do the believers behave to each other?
- What words explain their attitude?
- What is Jesus doing through this group?

The believers were "together", which means they spent time with each other. They also had everything "in common". This is the idea of "fellowship" or sharing. For example, they sold their things and gave to other people. This was not needed to join the community (not everyone sold their possessions or property). It was how people cared for each other in the community.

The believers met together regularly in the temple and in each other's homes. They were "glad" or joyful people because of what God had done for them. They were "sincere"; it was from their heart. They praised God for all he had done.

"Enjoying the favour of all the people" can mean they were treated well by the people around them. But a better translation is: "Having grace for all the people". The believers showed kindness to all those around them.

The Lord Jesus continued to work among them. He brought more new believers into the group. They were "being saved" by believing in Jesus.

Find the main point of the passage

- What do these verses teach us about church life?
- What do they tell us is important in a group of believers?

These verses tell us what should be important for God's people. It is a picture of how God's people should live together and what they should do. Their new life means a new relationship with God and with each other. So they learn about God, remember Jesus, praise God and pray to him. They also live together with other believers. They care for each other and encourage each other. This includes practical help and support.

So the main point of the passage is: Believers live out a new life together.

 PLAN

Main point of the sermon

A sermon explains the passage, and applies the passage to the hearers. Look at the main point of the passage. Write what this main point will mean for your hearers.

It will be something like this: Believers in Jesus live out their new life with God and each other.

Sub-points

- Read the main point again.
- Read the verses again.
- What sub-points will help you teach this passage?

This passage does not divide up easily. The themes are repeated through the passage. It is best to find the key themes and then explain them. You can use the themes of "new relationship with God", and "new relationship with each other".

Think of a heading for each sub-point.

For example:

1. New relationship with God (v42-43, 47)

2. New relationship with each other (v42, 44-46)

Illustrate

The main point is about the new community that believers are part of. For example, if you have new parents, that means you are in a new family and you have new brothers and sisters. So when we believe in Jesus, we have God as our new father and other believers as our brothers and sisters. That means we now live differently with them.

Apply

- In your church life what are the most important things?
- What needs to change so that your church has the same priorities as this first church?
- What can we learn so we can live together better as God's people?

How this applies will depend on your church. Which of these priorities is your church good at: The apostles' teaching, fellowship, the breaking of bread or prayer? Encourage people to keep going in those. Which of these priorities is your church bad at? Challenge people about those.

Review

Check the main point is clear and that you keep to THIS passage.

 # TEACH

Start

This passage is about the new community of the church. The new community is people who have repented and believed in Jesus. We will see what a community is like when people have been forgiven and are filled with God's Spirit.

Explain

New relationship with God (v42-43, 47)

When anyone believes in Jesus, they turn to God. They are forgiven and receive the Holy Spirit. How do they now live out their new relationship with God?

- They keep learning: They spend time learning from the apostles so they understand more about what God has done and promised. We can do this as we study the Bible and listen to teaching from God's word.
- They keep remembering: They remember Jesus' death for them by breaking bread together. Do we do this often and with joy?
- They keep praying: They praise and thank God. They ask him to bring more people to know him.

New relationship with each other (v42, 44-46)

There is also a new relationship with each other. Believers are united (joined together). *Use the illustration about joining a new family.* People give themselves to "fellowship"— their new, shared life. They learn together, eat together, remember together, and pray together. They spend time together and care for each other. They share their houses and possessions with each other.

The result was that Jesus brought new believers to join the group.

Apply

Encourage people with what a beautiful picture this is. This is a happy and united group of people. God is at work. How can we be more like this?

Encourage people about which of these they are doing well. Challenge people about which of these you need to do more in your situation.

End

God has made a new community of his people, who are his family. They live a new life with him and with each other.

Pray

Pray that your church will become more like this first church. Ask God to use you to bring more people to know Jesus as Lord and Saviour.

⬆ STUDY
POINTING TO JESUS

Background

Many people believed in Jesus. They formed a new community. The apostles did many signs and wonders (2:43). This passage tells us about one of those signs and what happens as a result.

Read

READ Acts 3:1-26 two or three times

Try to summarise each paragraph in your own words.

Understand

READ Acts 3:1-10

Verse 2: "Lame", "crippled from birth" – unable to walk.

Verse 2: "Beg" – ask for money.

- What are we told about the lame man who cannot walk?
- What does Luke emphasise in verses 7-10?

Peter and John meet a lame man who is begging. Peter heals him in the name of Jesus. Luke emphasises that he is healed immediately. He now walks and jumps! People are amazed.

READ Acts 3:11-16

Verse 13: "Glorified" – show someone is special.

Verse 14: "Disowned" – reject.

- How does Peter explain this healing?
- Find all the ways that Peter says people treated Jesus.
- Find the names Peter uses for Jesus.

Peter says that this healing was not done by himself or John. God did the miracle to give honour to Jesus. Notice that Peter calls God: "the God of Abraham, Isaac and Jacob, the God of our fathers" (v13). The God of the Old Testament has worked through Jesus.

Peter explains what the people have done. He says how terrible it is. They disowned Jesus, who was God's "Holy and Righteous One" (v14). They killed the "author" (giver) of life (v15).

But God raised Jesus from the dead. It is through Jesus that Peter can heal this lame man. So the healing is a sign of what God has done through Jesus. Miracles are meant to point people to Jesus.

READ verses 17-26

Verse 18: "Fulfilled" – made promises come true.

Verse 18: "Foretold" – said it will happen.

Verse 19: "Repent" – change direction.

Verse 25, 26: "Blessed" / "bless" – bring goodness and happiness.

- What is Peter's conclusion in verse 18?
- What does Peter tell people to do in verse 19? How does all this fit with the Old Testament (v22-26)?

God fulfilled all his promises in the Old Testament through what happened to Jesus. God said his Messiah (or Christ) would suffer to bring forgiveness (eg: Isaiah 53).

The people must now repent and turn to God. If they do, they will be forgiven. There will be times of refreshing—new life in the Holy Spirit. They will then wait for Jesus to return and restore the world.

All that happened fits with the Old Testament. Jesus is the new prophet that Moses talked about (v22). Everyone must now respond to Jesus (v23). Jesus' death and resurrection fulfils all that the prophets said would happen (v24-25).

Through Jesus, God kept his promise to Abraham to bring blessing (salvation) to all people (Genesis 12:3 and 22:18). This message came first to the Jews (v26), but then to the rest of the world.

Find the main point of the passage

- What does Peter say the people have done?
- What does Peter say God has done in Jesus?
- What should people now do?

The people rejected Jesus, who was God's Saviour. But that was part of God's plan to save people. Now he has shown who Jesus is by a miracle. This fulfils all that God promised in the Old Testament. People should now turn to Jesus to be forgiven.

So the main point is that God shows by a miracle what he has done in Jesus. Everyone should now turn to Jesus for forgiveness.

 **PLAN**

Main point of the sermon

A sermon explains the passage, and applies the passage to the hearers. Look at the main point of the passage. Write down what this main point will mean for your hearers.

It will be something like this: A miracle points to Jesus. Jesus is God's Saviour, who fulfils all God's promises. Everyone must turn to God and trust in Jesus for forgiveness.

Sub-points

- Read the main point again.
- Read the verses again.
- What sub-points will help you teach this passage?

This passage divides into two parts: The story of the healing, and how Peter explains it.

- How can you show what God has done in Jesus?
- How can you tell people what they should now do?

Think of a heading for each sub-point.

For example:

1. A miraculous sign (v1-10)

2. A wonderful Saviour (v11-16)

3. So turn and trust in Jesus (v17-26)

Illustrate

The main point is about realising who Jesus is. The miracle is a sign that points to him. Talk about road signs. They point us in the right direction. They tell us where to go. This passage is about a sign which points to Jesus and tells us what to do.

Apply

If we were alive when this happened, then we would respond to Jesus in the same way as these people did. Think about how the people rejected Jesus. We do the same too! We should feel ashamed because of our sin.

But God has worked through Jesus to bring forgiveness. We can be happy and excited.

We must know how important it is for people to turn to God and trust in Jesus. We must do this ourselves. We must help other people to do this.

Review

Check the main point is clear and that you keep to THIS passage.

 TEACH

Start

This passage is about understanding who Jesus is. It begins with a sign that points to Jesus. *Use your illustration.* Signs point us in the right direction and tell us where to go. This sign points to Jesus.

Explain

A miraculous sign (v1-10)

Explain the amazing miracle in v1-10. Show the sudden change and how everyone is amazed. Are you amazed? Then you are ready to hear how Peter explains the miracle.

A wonderful Saviour (v11-16)

This miracle does not mean Peter or John are special (v11-12). It is a sign but it does not point to them! Verse 13 is key: This miracle is a sign to show how special Jesus is.

The people made a terrible mistake in not understanding Jesus. They rejected and killed him, even though Jesus was God's servant. We would do the same if we were there.

But God raised Jesus from the dead. Jesus is alive and reigns with God. This miracle in Jesus' name is a sign pointing to Jesus, saying that Jesus is the Saviour sent by God.

So turn and trust in Jesus (v17-26)

The people listening to Peter must see who Jesus is. They must turn and trust in Jesus: So must we.

Explain that "repentance" means turning from sinful ways to God, so that he is Lord of your life. When someone repents, all their sin is cleaned away for ever. That person receives the Holy Spirit and lives for God, looking forward to when Jesus will return to restore everything.

God promised all this in the Old Testament. God promised to bless the world (v25). All God's promises are made true in Jesus. God's plan focuses on Jesus.

Apply

The miracle points us to Jesus, the Saviour. Do we know our sin in rejecting Jesus? Do we see who Jesus is? *Call people to believe in Jesus.*

End

Jesus is the one God sent to save. Although we have sinned, we can find forgiveness and peace in him. We must confess our sin, turn to God and trust in Jesus.

Pray

Pray that your people will understand all God has done in Jesus. Pray that you will rejoice in his forgiveness and live with Jesus as Lord, looking forward to his return.

⬆ STUDY
SPEAK FOR JESUS

Background

Peter healed a lame man and explained how this pointed to Jesus. In this passage we continue the story. We see the start of opposition from the Jewish religious leaders.

Read

READ Acts 4:1-22 two or three times.

Try to summarise the story in your own words.

Understand

READ Acts 4:1-4

Verse 1: "Priests" – some of the Jewish religious leaders.

Verse 1: "Temple guard" – the temple police.

Verse 1: "Sadducees" – a Jewish group who were some of the religious leaders.

- How do the Jewish leaders feel about the apostles' teaching? Why?
- So what do they do?

The religious leaders of the Jews are very annoyed about what the apostles are teaching. The apostles are teaching the people that Jesus rose from the dead. Some of the leaders believe in the resurrection, but they think it will only happen at God's final judgment. They don't think Jesus rose from the dead. They put Peter and John in prison. But more people believe in Jesus.

READ verses 5-12

Verse 6: "High priest" – the most important of the Jewish religious leaders.

Verse 12: "Salvation" – rescue from God's anger at sin.

- Who is at the meeting in verses 5-6? Why do you think Luke tells us about all these people?
- How does Peter answer their question in verse 7? (See v8-12.)
- What does Peter say about salvation in verse 12?

All of the important religious leaders meet together. Peter and John could easily be afraid. But Peter is filled with the Holy Spirit. This means Peter can answer boldly. Jesus promised the Holy Spirit would do this (Luke 12:11-12). Peter repeats what he said in chapter 3. The man was healed by Jesus. The leaders killed Jesus, but God raised him from the dead.

Peter quotes Psalm 118:22. This is about the king of Israel. It uses the picture of a stone that is thrown away. That stone is then put in the most important place: It becomes the capstone, or cornerstone. The person who was rejected is now put in the highest place. That is what happened to Jesus.

This means that salvation (forgiveness of sins) is through Jesus and no one else. There is no other way to be made right with the holy God. Peter wants to talk about Jesus—not about the healing.

READ verses 13-22

Verse 13: "Unschooled" – not trained in religion.

Verse 15: "Sanhedrin" – the ruling group of religious leaders.

- How do the Jewish leaders respond to Peter and John?
- What do they decide to do?
- How does Peter answer?

The leaders are amazed at the courage of Peter and John. They cannot tell them they are wrong because the man is healed. They discuss the problem together. They can see that a miracle happened. But they do not want the message about Jesus to spread. So they command Peter and John not to speak in the name of Jesus.

Peter and John refuse. They will listen to God—not to the leaders. They must speak about what they have seen and know about Jesus. The leaders cannot do anything because everyone knows an amazing miracle happened.

Find the main point of the passage

- What does this passage tell us about the religious leaders?
- What does this passage tell us about Jesus?
- What does this passage tell us about speaking for Jesus?

The religious leaders want to stop the message about Jesus from spreading. But Jesus is the only one who can save us. The apostles know that everyone needs to hear about Jesus.

So the main point is that we must speak about Jesus.

 **PLAN**

Main point of the sermon

A sermon explains the passage, and applies the passage to the hearers. Look at the main point of the passage. Write what this main point will mean for your hearers.

It will be something like this: We must speak the truth about Jesus and tell people that Jesus is the only way we can be saved from our sin. We must speak even when people are against us.

Sub-points

- Read the main point again.
- Read the verses again.
- What sub-points will help you teach this passage?

The passage divides into verses 1-4 about the opposition; then verses 5-12 about Peter's reply; then verses 13-22 about the Jewish leaders' response and Peter's reply.

Think of a heading for each sub-point.

For example:

1. Expect opposition to Jesus (v1-4)

2. Speak the truth about Jesus (v5-12)

3. Obey God, not people (v13-22)

Illustrate

The main point is about speaking the truth about Jesus, even when people are against us. Give examples of people who were brave in speaking about Jesus. For example in China, Iraq and Indonesia many pastors continue to speak the truth about Jesus even when they are told they will go to prison if they don't stop.

Apply

Do not be surprised if people oppose the truth about Jesus. Do not be afraid to speak the truth. God's Spirit can help you and make you bold.

Remember to obey God, not people. That may mean speaking about Jesus even if we are told not to. Ask God to guide you about what is right to do.

We must tell people that forgiveness for sin is only found in Jesus. We must do that even when people do not agree with us. That means we must know the truth ourselves. And we must be wise and loving.

Review

Check the main point is clear and that you keep to THIS passage.

 **TEACH**

Start

This passage is about speaking the truth about Jesus. Begin by talking about speaking for Jesus in your situation. It may be against the law of your country. People may feel afraid to speak the truth about Jesus. Use your illustration.

Explain

Expect opposition to Jesus (v1-4)

Explain the response of the religious leaders in verses 1-3. This is the start of opposition and it will get stronger. The message of Jesus tells us truth, which some people will not like. So there will be opposition.

Speak the truth about Jesus (v5-12)

Explain that perhaps Peter and John felt afraid. Show how the Holy Spirit gave them strength to speak. Peter is not afraid to speak about Jesus. He tells people what they need to know. Peter says that the leaders killed Jesus, but God raised Jesus from the dead. Peter knows for sure that Jesus is the only Saviour. Everyone should turn to trust in the name of Jesus.

Obey God, not people (v13-22)

Explain the reaction of the leaders. The leaders do not want the message about Jesus to spread. So they command Peter and John to stop talking about Jesus. But Peter and John will obey God, not the leaders. There are times when we should disobey leaders. We must disobey them when they tell us to do something which disobeys God.

Apply

We must not be surprised if the message about Jesus brings opposition. Some people will be against those who speak the message of Jesus.

We must tell people the truth about Jesus even when they do not want us to. We must obey God, not people. That may mean speaking about Jesus even if we are told not to. Sometimes it is right to disobey our government to speak about Jesus.

Jesus is the only way to be saved. So we must keep on telling people the good news about Jesus.

End

Jesus is the only way to be saved. We must speak about him.

Pray

Pray that you and your church will be bold to speak about Jesus.

↑ STUDY
PRAY FOR BOLDNESS

Background

This passage finishes the story which started in chapter 3. We saw the miracle of a lame man walking and heard the message about Jesus. The Jewish leaders were not happy. But Peter and John knew they must keep speaking about Jesus. Now we see how the believers pray.

Read

READ Acts 4:23-31 two or three times.

Say the meaning of each verse in your own words.

Understand

READ verse 23

- Where do Peter and John go?
- What do they say?
- How may this group feel?

Peter and John go back to "their own people"—the people who believe in Jesus. Peter and John tell them what happened in verses 18-21. Some believers may feel afraid. Some may want to stop speaking about Jesus.

READ verses 24-30

Verse 24: "Sovereign" – the one who rules over everything.

Verse 25: "Plot in vain" – make useless plans.

Verse 26: "Anointed one" – God's Messiah or chosen one.

Verse 27: "Conspire" – plan or plot.

- Why do the believers begin by speaking about God as Sovereign and Creator in verse 24, do you think?
- Where do they quote from in v25-26?
- How do they see Psalm 2 fulfilled in the death of Jesus?
- What do they ask God to do?

They begin their prayer remembering God is the Ruler and the Creator. So they remember that God is in control. This is why they call God "Sovereign Lord".

They quote Psalm 2. Psalm 2 is about rulers who go against God and his Messiah. Psalm 2 is fulfilled in the opposition to Jesus. People planned against Jesus (Acts 4:27). But what happened was what God "decided beforehand should happen" (v28). God was in control. So the believers remind themselves that God is in control. They know that opposition does not mean God's plans have gone wrong.

They ask God to "consider [the] threats" of the people who are against them (v29). They ask God to take notice. They pray God will help them speak the message about Jesus. They ask that they will speak it boldly, without fear, as Peter did. They also ask God to do miracles and signs in the name of Jesus. These signs go with speaking about Jesus. That is what happened with the healing of the lame man. They ask God for what happened in chapters 3 – 4 to happen again!

READ verse 31

- What happens after they pray?
- What is the result?

The place is "shaken". God shows them that he heard their prayer. They are filled with the Holy Spirit. This means they speak the message about Jesus boldly, without fear. This is the same as what happened to Peter (v8).

Extra

This passage raises questions about miracles today. Should we pray for miracles as the believers did then? See the extra section after this study.

Find the main point of the passage

- What does this passage tell us about going against God?
- What does this passage tell us about how to respond to opposition?
- What is the main lesson from these verses?

The believers pray to God. They remember God is in control. They ask for God's help to keep speaking about Jesus.

So the main point is that God is in control. We should ask for his help to keep speaking about Jesus.

PLAN

Main point of the sermon

A sermon explains the passage, and applies the passage to the hearers. Look at the main point of the passage. Write what this main point will mean for your hearers.

People go against Jesus and oppose the good news about him. When this happens we must remember that God is in control. We must pray for boldness to keep speaking about Jesus.

Sub-points

- Read the main point again.
- Read the verses again.
- What sub-points will help you teach this passage?

This passage is about praying when people are against the message of Jesus. The prayer has two main parts:

- Reminder of God's control
- Prayer for boldness

Think of headings for the sub-points.

For example:

When people are against you for speaking about Jesus:

1. Remember God is in control (v23-28)

2. Pray to speak without fear (v29-31)

Illustrate

When believers know God is in control, they want to keep speaking about Jesus. God is the boss over everything (the "Sovereign Lord"). Soldiers in the army always obey the commanding officer. If someone tells them to do something different, who will they obey? God is the commanding officer for believers. God is in control. Believers must obey God, not other people.

Apply

How do people go against you for speaking about Jesus? Do any government authorities tell you not to? Do people respond badly when you speak about Jesus?

What does speaking about Jesus without fear mean in your place? What will happen if you are too afraid to share God's message?

How do you respond if people go against your message about Jesus? Do you get angry? Do you stop? Or do you follow the example of the believers in Acts?

Review

Check the main point is clear and that you keep to THIS passage.

 # TEACH

Start

You may talk about how you face opposition in your situation. You can use verse 23 to link to the passage. Explain what happened in verses 1-22. Ask people to think how the believers might feel when they are commanded never to speak the message about Jesus.

Explain

When people are against you for speaking about Jesus:

1. Remember God is in control (v23-28)

The believers were told not to speak about Jesus. They responded by praying. This passage tells us how to pray.

We must remind ourselves that God is in control of everything. This helps us to obey God and not people. *Use your illustration.*

Explain the quote from Psalm 2. The worst opposition to God was opposition to Jesus. But that was only what God said would happen. God knows about all hatred and opposition before it happens. This reminds us that God is in control, and reminds us to trust him.

2. Pray to speak without fear (v29-31)

The believers ask for boldness to keep on speaking. They ask God to do signs and miracles. *Explain why we must have a different understanding about signs and miracles today (see extra p52).* We must ask God to help us to speak boldly. That will mean speaking when we do not want to. It will mean saying things people do not like.

Apply

This passage challenges believers when people are against us. We must remember that God is in control, and ask for boldness to keep on speaking about Jesus.

It also helps us. Because God is in control, believers do not have to worry or fear. It means we can keep speaking confidently, with courage, about Jesus.

If you are not a believer, then you need to realise that you are not on God's side. You are against God. He sent Jesus to rescue you. Will you turn to him?

End

God is in control so we must ask for God's help to speak boldly and without fear about Jesus.

Pray

Pray that you and your church will respond in this way to those who are against the message of God.

EXTRA

Discussion on miracles

In Acts we see the apostles doing many miracles. These are usually healing people. This raises a question: Should we expect the same miracles today?

Look at the following verses and think what they tell us about miracles:

READ Acts 2:43, 3:6-7, 5:12-16

The miracles were done by the apostles. They were able to heal immediately and completely. They healed all the people who came to them. This is the same sort of healing as Jesus did.

Later in Acts, people other than the apostles do similar healings (see Acts 8:6-7). But most are done by the apostles. In chapter 9 we see an example of someone who has died. The believers do not pray for her to rise from the dead. They send for Peter (an apostle) so he can pray for her.

This fits with what Jesus said about the apostles. Jesus said he would give them special power because they would witness and speak for him (Luke 24:49, Acts 1:8). Later the apostle Paul said that doing miracles is one of the marks of an apostle:

"I persevered in demonstrating among you the marks of a true apostle, including signs, wonders and miracles." (2 Corinthians 12:12)

So what we see is this: As the good news first spread, God gave his apostles the ability to perform miracles as signs, and sometimes other people did this as well.

READ Acts 14:3, Hebrews 2:3-4

■ What do these verses tell us that miracles are for?

First, miracles show people that the message is true. God confirms the message through his apostles by giving these signs.

We must also remember that Jesus warned people not to only look for signs (see Matthew 12:39, 16:4). God gives signs to confirm his message. God does not give signs to people who demand proof.

So the miracles done in Acts were to confirm the message about Jesus. Miracles were mostly done by the apostles because they were his chosen witnesses. That does not mean miracles do not happen today, but we should not expect them in the same way.

God may again decide to confirm his message and show his power through miracles. So we can pray for healing. But God has not promised to do this. So we cannot be sure God will do it. We must expect a difference between the church today and the believers in Acts.

⬆ STUDY
TRUE COMMUNITY

Background

We read about the life of believers in Acts 2:42-47. This passage tells us more about their life together. The believers were opposed by Jewish authorities outside the church. They now have problems inside the church. This passage shows us what they did about these problems.

Read

🡲 **READ** 4:32 – 5:11 two or three times.

Put each verse into your own words.

Understand

🡲 **READ** verses 32-35

Verse 32: "One in heart and mind" – completely united.

Verse 33: "Testify" – be a witness.

Verse 33: "God's grace" – free kindness that they did not deserve.

- What are the believers like?
- What are the apostles doing?
- How is God's grace seen in this community?

The believers are united as one group. This shows in the way they share their things. They do not keep possessions to themselves, but share with each other. They don't have to do this in order to join the community or become a believer. It is what people want to do, to care for those in need. It is a sign of their love and unity. Caring for each other is part of following Jesus (see John 13:34-35).

The apostles continue to testify (or "witness", see Acts 1:8) to Jesus' resurrection. This is what we already saw them doing. The result is that God's grace—his free kindness—is in them. We see the grace of God at work in how they care for each other.

🡲 **READ** verses 36-37

Verse 36: "Encouragement" – to strengthen people.

- What do we learn about Barnabas?

Barnabas is an example of someone who sold land to care for believers. He is very different from Ananias and Sapphira. He will be an important person later in Acts.

🡲 **READ** 5:1-11

Verse 4: "Your disposal" – yours to use as you wanted.

Verse 5, 11: "Seized" – took hold of.

Verse 9: "Conspire" – plan or plot.

- What do Ananias and Sapphira do wrong?
- Why does God judge them immediately?

- What does God want to see in the community of believers?

Ananias and Sapphira sell land to care for the poor. But they keep part of the money for themselves. Peter says the land belonged to them, and the money was theirs. They did not have to give all the money away. What they did wrong was to pretend they had given all of it.

Peter says Ananias "lied to the Holy Spirit", and "lied ... to God" (verse 3, 4). Ananias and Sapphira try to trick God so that they will look good to the people. Peter says that Satan is behind this (verse 3), but they are still responsible. Satan wants to disturb and spoil the Christian community.

God punishes for this immediately. People have done similar things since and were not immediately killed. God probably punished Ananias and Sapphira immediately to show that he hates deceit and lies in his people. God had an important lesson to teach this young church.

Find the main point of the passage

- What does this passage teach about what is important in church life?
- What does this passage teach we must not do?
- What does God want to see in his church?
- What does God not want in his church?
- What is the main lesson from these verses?

God wants to see his people caring for each other. God wants to see kindness, giving and love. God hates to see the opposite. God hates to see people deceiving each other. God hates to see people trying to look good.

So the main point is that God loves to see caring community and hates to see tricks and lies.

 PLAN

Main point of the sermon

A sermon explains the passage, and applies it to your hearers. Look at the main point of the passage. Write what this main point will mean for your hearers.

For example: God loves to see a true caring community. God hates to see deceit and lies in his people.

Sub-points

- Read the main point again.
- Read the verses again.
- What sub-points will help you teach this passage?

This passage is about the life of the church—those who believe in Jesus. It gives us a good example of caring for others unselfishly. It gives a bad example of how lies spoil God's church.

Think of a heading for each sub-point.

For example:

1. God loves to see a caring community (4:32-37)

2. God hates to see lies and tricks in community (5:1-11)

Illustrate

Use real-life illustrations that you know about. For example, people you know who cared for other Christians. Or people who gave money or their things. Use some good examples. This is like a family. We share our things with our family, and we must share with our Christian brothers and sisters.

Also use some bad examples. (Don't use names.) Speak about people who wanted to look better than they were and so tricked and lied to others.

Apply

Do people care for each other in your church? Do people unselfishly share and look after each other? Is your Christian community of one heart and mind? What needs to change?

What lies and tricks do you need to be careful of? Are there ways that people try to look good to others? Are we completely honest with God and with others?

This means there must never be stealing or borrowing church money. Church funds must never be used for something and the church told something different. False reports about money must never be given.

Review

Check the main point is clear and that you keep to THIS passage.

 # TEACH

Start

What do people love to see in their children? Kindness, truth, love.

What do people hate to see in their children? Lies, being selfish.

This passage is about the community of God's people. It tells us what God loves to see in his community. It shows what God hates to see.

Explain

1. God loves to see a caring community (4:32-37)

The first church was joined together like a happy family. People cared for each other practically. *Make clear that this was a free choice.* The result was that no one was in need. God loves to see this in his people. *Show how Barnabas is an example.*

This love and care is connected to the message of Jesus. In the middle of telling us about church life, Luke tells us of the apostles witnessing to Jesus' resurrection. Understanding and being thankful for God's work in Jesus is what makes this community behave like this. It is all because of God's grace and kindness.

2. God hates to see lies and tricks in community (5:1-11)

Explain what Ananias and Sapphira did wrong. The problem was they pretended to give all the money.

They wanted people to think they were good. They lied to the people. They lied to God.

Explain why God judged them for their lies. This shows how God feels about lies and tricks. God hates to see lies in his community. *Explain that God does not usually judge immediately in this way today.* But we know how God feels about people who try to look good to others but lie to him. It is very serious to do things like this.

Apply

Warn people about how we try to look good. That can be in giving money or in other ways.

Challenge people about how willing they are to share. God loves to see us sharing. God loves to see no one in need among his people. *Use your illustration.* We need God's grace to be at work in us so that we are one and care for each other.

End

Work towards being a true loving community and change your behaviour where you do wrong.

Pray

Pray that you and your church will be one and care for each other.

⬆ STUDY
NOTHING WILL STOP THE MESSAGE

Background

In chapter 4 the religious leaders told Peter and John not to speak about Jesus. Then the believers asked God to do more signs and miracles and to give them boldness to keep on speaking about Jesus. In this passage God answers their prayer.

Read

READ Acts 5:12-42 two or three times.

Put each verse in your own words.

Understand

READ verses 12-16

Verse 12: "Solomon's Colonnade/Porch" – a part of the temple building.

- What main events happen?
- How do people think about the group of believers?
- What is the result?

The apostles do "signs and wonders". These are miracles of healing (see "Extra" on p52). There is interest and fear from people. They see something different and attractive about the church but they are afraid of joining. The news spreads and people come from villages all around.

READ verses 17-26

Verse 17: "Sadducees" – one of the Jewish religious groups.

Verse 18: "Jail" – prison.

Verse 21: "Sanhedrin" – the ruling council of the Jews.

- How do the religious leaders react to the apostles?
- Why does God get the apostles out of prison?
- What is funny about verses 21-26?

The religious leaders are jealous. They tried to stop this message about Jesus spreading. But now it is spreading more and more. They put the apostles in prison to stop them.

God does not get the apostles out of prison so they can run away. God gets them out to continue preaching (v20). This shows that God wants everyone to hear the message of "new life" in Jesus.

The next day the guards cannot find the apostles! Someone tells the leaders the apostles are preaching in the temple. They are doing the very thing the leaders tried to stop! The Jewish council is made to look powerless. They cannot stop this message spreading.

The apostles still go on trial in front of the Sanhedrin. The escape from prison only meant they could preach for a while. It shows God is in control and God will make sure the message of Jesus spreads.

READ verses 27-42

Verse 31: "Exalted" – lifted to a high position of authority.

Verse 31: "Prince" – ruler or lord.

Verse 40: "Flogged/whipped' – beaten with ropes.

Verse 41: "Disgrace" – shame.

- How does Peter answer the Sanhedrin (v 29-32)?
- Why are the council very angry ("furious")?
- What is Gamaliel's advice? How should we understand it?

Peter and the other apostles say they must obey God rather than people. God has made Jesus "Prince" or "Ruler", and "Saviour" (v31). This means people must repent and come to Jesus and ask him for forgiveness. They challenge the Sanhedrin to do this. That is why the Sanhedrin are so angry and want to kill them (v33).

Gamaliel advises to do nothing. He reminds them of other uprisings. Once the leader was dead the rebellion stopped. So Gamaliel says this will stop. But if it is from God, then they must not oppose it because they will be fighting God.

We have seen that this is from God. The apostles know this. So they rejoice to suffer for Jesus (v40, 41). And they keep on speaking about Jesus the Messiah (v42).

Find the main point of the passage

- What does this passage show about God's authority?
- What does this passage teach about how God wants the message of Jesus to spread?

God controls the spread of the message about Jesus. God will make sure people will hear it. No one can stop it spreading even if they are in a position of authority.

So the main point is that nothing can stop God's message spreading.

 PLAN

Main point of the sermon

Write your main point.

It will be something like this: The spread of the message of Jesus will never be stopped because this is from God.

Sub-points

- Read the main point again.
- Read the verses again.
- What sub-points will help you teach this passage?

This passage is about the spread of the good news about Jesus. God wants the message of new life in Jesus to spread. Because this is from God, no one can stop the message about Jesus spreading.

Think of a heading for each sub-point.

For example:

1. The message about Jesus is from God (v12-20)

2. Be careful not to go against God's message (v21-39)

3. Keep on speaking the good news of Jesus (v40-42)

Illustrate

The spread of the good news can be illustrated by stories. For example, in China when the communist government tried to stop the spread of the good news, people were very worried about what would happen. They thought the church might die. But years later there were many more believers! The message had spread much further.

Or use the illustration of a fire. People try to stop the fire spreading and stamp it out, just as they do with the message of the gospel. But it is like God is blowing on the message. He will make sure it spreads—as the wind spreads fire.

Apply

Warn those who are against the message of Jesus. God has made Jesus Ruler and Saviour. Every person needs to turn away from their sins and ask for forgiveness. If they do not, they will be fighting against God.

Be confident that this message of Jesus is from God. God will make sure it keeps on spreading. Be confident in telling people the good news. When people try to stop the spreading, they will fail. God's message WILL continue to grow.

Review

Check the main point is clear and that you keep to THIS passage.

 # TEACH

Start

Tell of the spread of the message of Jesus in your area or country. How do your people feel about telling others the good news of Jesus? Are they afraid or worried? If your people are good at drama, you could get them to practise and present a drama of this story.

Explain

As we read this story, think what it was like to be one of the apostles, or a member of the Jewish Council. How would you feel?

The message about Jesus is from God (v12-20)
God confirms the message of the apostles by signs and miracles. Think of the excitement as people lying on their beds are healed! This shows this is God's message.

The religious leaders try to stop the message spreading by putting the apostles in prison. But God gets them out again. *Explain what happens in verses 19-21.* God does not get them out so that they can run away. God gets them out because he wants the message of new life to spread to everyone. God shows that he is in control. Think what it was like to be one of the apostles.

Be careful not to go against God's message (v21-39)
The religious leaders meet the next morning. But the prisoners cannot be found! The apostles are telling people the good news about Jesus. *Show how the leaders are made to look silly!*

The leaders question the apostles (v27-28). *Explain the reply of the apostles (v29-32).* God has made Jesus the Ruler and Saviour. Everyone must now repent and ask Jesus for forgiveness. The apostles are witnesses to this and so is the Holy Spirit. God is working.

What does this mean for the religious leaders? They should stop going against this message, and see what God has done in Jesus.

Explain Gamaliel's advice (v34-39). If this new movement is from people, it will stop by itself. If it is from God, no one will be able to stop it. Encourage Christians to see that nothing will stop the message of Jesus. People who oppose it are against God.

Keep on speaking the good news of Jesus (v40-42)
The apostles were beaten up. They were ordered never to speak about Jesus. But that did not stop them! They were willing to suffer for Jesus. They rejoiced in suffering. The apostles kept on speaking the good news. They "never stopped teaching and proclaiming the good news" (v42).

10

Apply

Encourage people that the good news cannot be stopped because it is from God. That does not mean there will always be success. In this passage the apostles suffer. But it does mean we know the message of Jesus will keep spreading. God wants everyone to know the wonderful message of new life. *Give your illustration.*

Warn people not to oppose God. Call people to turn away from their sin and trust in Jesus for forgiveness.

Encourage people to keep on spreading the message of Jesus. We must keep on telling people the good news that Jesus is the Saviour. We must be willing to suffer for doing this.

End

God's message is powerful. Nothing will stop it, so spread the good news yourself.

Pray

Pray that you and your hearers will be confident and keep on speaking God's message.

STUDY
MOST IMPORTANT

Background

This passage returns to how the first believers lived together and cared for each other. We have seen this two times already (2:42-47 and 4:32-5:11). But now there is a problem with caring for so many people in the church. What will the believers do?

Read

READ verses 6:1-7 two or three times.

Put each verse into your own words.

Understand

READ verse 1

Verse 1: "Hellenistic Jews"/"Grecian Jews" – Jews who spoke Greek and did not usually live in Israel.

Verse 1: "Hebraic Jews" – Jews who spoke Hebrew and lived in Israel.

Verse 1: "Overlooked" – left out or ignored.

- What is the problem?
- Why do you think this has happened?
- Why is it such a big problem?

Some of the widows in the church are left out when the food is shared. They are from the group of "Hellenistic Jews". There may be favouritism between these groups or even racism. Or maybe there were too many people to manage.

This was a big problem. God's people are not to favour one group or person above another. God's people must care for everyone equally and be one. This was not happening.

READ verses 2-6

Verse 2: "The Twelve" – the twelve apostles.

Verse 2, 4: "The ministry of the word" – proclaiming and teaching God's message.

Verse 2: "Wait on tables" – distribute food.

- How do the apostles respond to this problem?
- What does this show about what is most important in the life of the church?
- How is the whole group of believers part of this process?

The apostles must focus on prayer and teaching God's word. But they think it is essential that some good people organise the food sharing. Teaching and prayer are important for them. But it is important that the problems with food are sorted out in a good and fair way.

The group of believers are led by the apostles but are part of the whole process. They choose good men to be in charge of this work. They are godly and wise men. The men chosen have Greek names. Probably many of them were from the Greek-speaking Jewish group. This shows wisdom in choosing leaders from the group that were left out.

READ verse 7

- What is the result of sorting out this problem?
- Why does Luke mention priests becoming believers here?

The result is that more and more people became believers. This includes some of the priests. One reason why Luke writes about this is to show that the message about Jesus is spreading well even among very committed Jews.

Sorting out the problem of care in the church is needed for the church to grow. If they don't sort out this problem, the lack of care in the church will make the message of Jesus weak. This passage shows the importance of Bible teachers continuing with preaching and prayer. It also shows we must care and show practical love for each other in the church.

Find the main point of the passage

- What does this passage tell us about what is important in church life?
- What does it teach about how to sort out problems in church life?
- What does it show about different people having different responsibilities?
- What does it tell us about who we give responsibilities to?

The passage focuses on putting right a problem of care among believers. It was important the problem was sorted out. It was sorted out by giving responsibility to suitable people. That meant the apostles could continue teaching and praying.

So this passage shows the importance of teaching God's word and also of caring for people.

PLAN

Main point of the sermon

Write your main point...

It will be something like: Teaching God's word and showing practical love are both very important.

Sub-points

- Read the main point again.
- Read the verses again.
- What sub-points will help you teach this passage?

This passage is about the life of the believers. It was not right for the apostles to leave the teaching of God's word and prayer. But it was also not right to ignore the problems with the food. There must be godly people put in charge of the food while the apostles continue teaching and praying.

Think of a heading for each sub-point.

- How can the sub-points connect together?
- How can they encourage people to make sure the important things are done well?

For example:

1. Teaching God's word and prayer are important (v1-4)

2. Practical love and care are important (v3, 5-7)

Illustrate

Think of parents bringing up their children. They must teach them God's word and pray for them. But they must also care for them practically, giving them food and clothes.

Or think about a business. Different people have different jobs and responsibilities. But all of the people are needed for the business to work properly. Or think of an example that connects with your people.

Apply

We must make teaching and prayer important in our churches. The people responsible for this (like church leaders) must be given enough time to do it well. They must not have lots of practical work as well.

We must make practical love and care important in our churches. We must make sure no one is forgotten or not cared for. We must make faithful, mature people responsible to make sure this is done well.

Review

Check the main point is clear and that you keep to THIS passage.

 TEACH

Start

Maybe talk about what people think is important in your church. We see what is important to a church in the way they sort out problems. That is what we see in this passage.

Explain

Introduction

Explain the problem (v1). One group is being left out. Before we were told they were "one in heart and mind", and that "there was no needy person" (4:32, 34).

What will the apostles do about this problem? What will it teach us about what is important in church life?

1. Teaching God's word and prayer are important (v1-4)

Explain the apostles' response (v2-4). They must not stop teaching God's word or praying. These are essential for the church to grow.

We do not have apostles, but we do have church leaders and others whose main work is teaching. They must not stop teaching and sort out practical problems in the church instead. We must encourage them to keep on teaching and praying.

2. Practical love and care is important (v3, 5-7)

The apostles do not ignore the problem. They find faithful and wise men who can sort out the problem.

Love and care in the life of the church is essential (John 13:34-35). This failure to love must be sorted out. *Illustrate with the picture of a family, where both instruction and care are needed.*

Churches need different people in charge of different parts of life. *Illustrate with different jobs in a business.* The apostles had one job, but other people will have the job of practical care. The result is the spread of the word of God (v7). When the church works well, the message about Jesus spreads.

Apply

How you apply will depend on what your church thinks is most important. If they believe only teaching is important, then challenge people with the need to love. If people think only love is important, then challenge them with the need for teaching God's word and prayer.

End

Both teaching God's word and love are essential to the church. The result is the good news spreads.

Pray

Pray that you and your church will be committed to both teaching God's word and showing practical love.

↑ STUDY
REJECTING GOD

Background

This passage starts a new section in the book of Acts (6:8 – 9:31). It looks at three different people. We see how God works in Stephen, Philip and Saul. We see the good news spread out from Jerusalem. The first passage looks at Stephen. This is when persecution against Christians gets much stronger.

This is a very long passage because Stephen makes a long speech, telling the story of God's Old Testament people.

Read

READ 6:8 – 7:60

Read it out loud at least once. Try to summarise each paragraph in your own words.

Understand

READ chapter 6:8-15

- What is Stephen like (v8,10)?
- What do some Jewish leaders say he did wrong?
- Why is this so serious?

God is using Stephen. But Stephen is wrongly accused of speaking against Moses and God (v11); and against the temple and the law (v13-14). These were the most important things in the Jewish religion.

- Think: Has Jesus changed the role of the law and temple (v14)?

Jesus said he did not come to destroy the law but to fulfil it (Matthew 5:17). Jesus changed things. But this is only because Jesus is what the temple and law pointed to.

READ chapter 7:1-50

Verse 8: "Patriarchs" – fathers of the Jews.

Stephen explains:

- God's call to Abraham (v2-8)
- Joseph being rejected and saving his family (v9-16)
- How Moses was rejected (v17-29)
- God choosing Moses to rescue his people (v30-36)
- God promising another prophet like Moses (v37-38)
- People rejecting Moses' leadership (v39-43)
- The tabernacle and temple (v44-50)

- How did his people respond to Moses (v23-29)?
- But who does Stephen say Moses was (v35-36)?
- How did people respond to God's law (v37-42)?
- How should people think about the temple (v44-50)?

Moses was rejected by his people

(v27). But they rejected the one God sent as their "ruler and deliverer" (v35).

Moses gave God's law to the people. But they refused to obey God's word through him (v39). We see this when they made the golden calf (v40-41). This is why the prophet Amos spoke about God's people worshipping idols (v42-43).

The tabernacle and the temple were very significant. But God is not limited to these buildings. As the prophet Isaiah said, God lives in the whole world (v48-50).

READ chapter 7:51-53

Verse 51: "Stiff-necked" – stubborn, like an animal which will not wear a harness.

Verse 51: "Uncircumcised" hearts and minds – not wanting to listen to God or obey God.

- What does Stephen accuse the Jewish people of?
- What examples does he give (v35,39)?
- Who is the Righteous One (v52)?
- What does Stephen say the people did?

Stephen says that God's people in the Old Testament always resisted God. They turned away from God and did not listen to what he said.

They rejected the people God sent to rescue them (like Moses). They rejected God's prophets. The people showed the same attitude in how they treated Jesus; they betrayed and killed him.

READ chapter 7:54-60

Verse 54: "Furious and gnashed their teeth" – very, very angry.

- How do people respond to Stephen?
- How does this show that what he just said is true?

The people listening are very angry. They want to stop Stephen's words and so they stone him. This is exactly what happened to the prophets, as Stephen said. So they show again they do not want to listen to God's message.

Find the main point of the passage

- What does this passage teach about how people respond to God?
- What is the main lesson from these verses?

The passage shows how God's Old Testament people always resisted him. Then we see it in how they rejected Jesus. So the main point is: People will reject what God has done in Jesus.

PLAN

Main point of the sermon

Write your main point.

For example: People keep turning away from God. We reject him and his Saviour: Jesus.

Sub-points

- Read the main point again.
- Read verses 51-53 again.
- What sub-points will help you teach this passage?

This passage contains a lot of Old Testament history. It is best to teach it by focusing on Stephen's conclusion in verses 51-53. This shows us that people rejected God's messengers and rescuers. This shows a wrong attitude to God—that we resist him (v51).

Think of a heading for each sub-point.

- How can we connect what the people of Israel did with ourselves today?

We need to remember that this tells us the history of God's people in the Old Testament. But it also explains how people respond to God in general. So when we look at Old Testament Israel, we see a warning for us not to do the same.

For example:

1. People reject God and his Saviour (6:8-15, 7:23-43)

2. Do not reject God yourself (7:51-60)

3. Warn others not to reject God (7:51-53)

Illustrate

Some children reject their parents and go against them. When their parents try to help them, they push them away. In the same way we do not listen to God. We reject God even when he tries to rescue us.

Apply

We must realise how bad our hearts are. We must see the ways that we reject God and his rescue in Jesus. When a friend or church leader tries to show us our sin, we must listen carefully. Do not reject God.

- What other ways do we reject God? Think of some examples for your people.
- Think how you can apply this passage to the unbelievers who will listen to you.

Review

Check the main point is clear and that you keep to THIS passage.

 # TEACH

Start

Talk about how people respond when we tell them they are wrong. They often get angry. This passage shows us what happens when Stephen tells people they are wrong about Jesus: they get very angry. These people show us what we are like.

Explain

Do not try to explain all of the speech.

1. People reject God and his Saviour (6:8-15, 7:23-43)

Explain how people start to speak against Stephen (6:8-14). He says God has brought a new salvation in Jesus. People do not want to hear this. Stephen explains himself in his speech.

Focus on what Stephen accuses the people of in 7:51-53. Show how he gave examples of this in his speech, especially the example of Moses. Show how people rejected Moses, who God sent to rescue his people (7:23-36). God promised to send another rescuer like Moses (7:37). Then from verse 52 show that people have rejected Jesus too.

2. Do not reject God yourself (7:51-60)

Our hearts turn away from God and reject his rescue. *Give examples of how we do this. Use your illustration.*

We disobey God's commands. We are proud and selfish.

We must not reject God. *Ask people if they are rejecting God. Explain ways they may be doing this. Ask them if they reject God's offer of rescue in Jesus. Do they close their ears and hearts to God?*

3. Warn others not to reject God (7:51-53)

We must warn people not to reject God. That is what Stephen did, and we must do the same. People may reject us as they rejected Stephen. We must be ready for persecution.

Apply

How do you respond when a friend or church leader shows that you are wrong? Remember that they may be warning of how you are against God and his ways. Listen with a humble heart.

End

This passage shows what we are really like. We must be sad about the way we reject God. We must be very thankful for God's patience. We must be careful not to reject him ourselves, and we must warn others.

Pray

Pray that you and your hearers will not reject God and will warn others.

⬆ STUDY
THE CHANGE JESUS BRINGS

Background

The good news of Jesus has been preached in Jerusalem but opposition has increased. Stephen was the first person to die for teaching about Jesus.

This passage shows how the message of Jesus spread out from Jerusalem. It tells about the first people who were not Jews who heard the good news about Jesus. It focuses on the complete change of life that Jesus brings to people.

Read

⟅ **READ** 8:1-13 two or three times.

Explain each verse in your own words.

Understand

⟅ **READ** verses 1-3

Verse 1: "Persecution" – suffering harm.

Verse 1: "Judea and Samaria" – the two regions around Jerusalem.

- What happens to the believers in Jerusalem?
- What does Saul start to do?

The believers in Jerusalem have to leave and live in other places. This

is because of persecution. A leader of this persecution is Saul. He tries to destroy the church, to stop it existing. Saul searches for people who believe in Jesus and puts them in prison.

⟅ **READ** verses 4-8

Verse 7: "Shrieks" – loud cries.

Verse 7: "Paralysed or lame" – people who cannot walk.

- What do the believers do as they are scattered?
- Explain what Philip does in Samaria.
- What happens in the city?

As the believers are scattered, they tell people about Jesus. So the result of persecution is that the message about Jesus spreads into new areas. This is what Jesus said would happen (see Acts 1:8).

Philip goes to Samaria. This used to be the northern kingdom of Israel in the Old Testament. The people who lived there had mixed with other races. So they were like "half-Jews". They followed a religion which was similar to the Jewish religion from the Old Testament, but also different. Philip tells them how Jesus is God's Saviour. He does miracles and so they listen to what he says.

The result is there is great joy in the city.

READ verses 9-13

- What kind of person is Simon?
- What does Simon think about himself (v9)?
- What effect does he have on the people in this city?
- What change happens because Philip preaches the message of Jesus (v12)?

Simon used evil power to do great things. He boasted he was a great person who people must listen to. Everyone gave him their attention. This included the most important people and the least people ("high and low"). They believed he had power from God (v10).

The writer, Luke, shows how they followed Simon (v11). Their lives put Simon at the centre. Luke then explains how Philip's preaching changes everything. Philip tells them the message about Jesus and the kingdom of God. "The kingdom of God" (v12) is how God is bringing the world back under his rule. God does that through Jesus. When a person turns to God and is forgiven, they enter the kingdom and have Jesus as their King.

The people hear this message, believe and are baptised. Baptism shows they believe the message and will now live with Jesus as King. So the good news means they stop living with Simon in control and start living with Jesus in control. Even Simon believes and is baptised.

Find the main point of the passage

- What does this passage say about the good news about Jesus spreading?
- How do people's lives change when they believe in Jesus?

God uses the persecution to spread the good news to Samaria. This was part of his plan (see 1:8). Many people stop following Simon the sorcerer and live joyfully with Jesus in control of their life.

So the main point is that people's lives are changed when they hear the good news about Jesus.

 **PLAN**

Main point of the sermon

Your sermon will explain the passage, and apply it to your hearers. Look at the main point of the passage. Write what this main point will mean for your hearers.

For example: The good news of Jesus spreads—and many people are changed to live with Jesus in control.

Sub-points

- Read the main point again.
- Read the verses again.
- What sub-points will help you teach this passage?

This passage is about the spread of the message about Jesus and the change he brings. God uses persecution to make the message spread out from Jerusalem. Philip tells people in Samaria about Jesus. People stop living with Simon at the centre of their lives. Jesus is at the centre instead.

Think of a heading for each sub-point.

For example:

1. The spread of the good news about Jesus (v1-8)

2. The change Jesus brings (v9-13)

Illustrate

Talk about someone you know whose life changed when they became a Christian. Before they became a Christian, money, power, success, or enjoyment were at the centre of their life. Now following Jesus, obeying Jesus, and serving Jesus are at the centre of their life.

Apply

Our whole life changes when we turn to Jesus. What was at the centre is replaced by Jesus. This means everything in life changes. We want to live for Jesus, obey Jesus and serve Jesus. So we live differently when we follow him. Is this true of you? Has your life been turned round by Jesus? Is he the centre of everything now?

Review

Check the main point is clear and that you keep to THIS passage.

 # TEACH

Start

Talk about how we all live for something. We all have something at the centre of our lives—money, power, success. For some people it will be religion—Islam, idols or ancestor worship. Ask people what is at the centre of their lives.

Explain

1. The spread of the good news about Jesus (v1-8)

The persecution is bad because it is hard for God's people. But God uses it. *Show how the persecution spread God's people into Judea and Samaria.* This was what Jesus said would happen (see 1:8).

Philip is an example of someone who told people the good news about Jesus. God wants his message about Jesus to spread across the world. This is still God's plan. We are part of that plan as we tell people about Jesus. God may use bad events like persecution for his message to spread through us.

2. The change Jesus brings (v9-13)

Explain how the people in Samaria lived before. Show how Simon was at the centre of their lives: They followed him. Explain that we all have something at the centre of our life that we follow. That may be a person like Simon, a thing like money, or a religion like Islam.

Philip told people about Jesus and the kingdom of God (v12). This is how God brings his rescue and rule through Jesus to people. People came to believe the good news about Jesus. They showed this by being baptised.

Even Simon the sorcerer believed. Instead of the people following him, he now follows Philip. This is a picture of the complete change the good news of Jesus brings.

Apply

Encourage people to spread the good news about Jesus. Encourage people that God may use hard times in our lives to make this to happen.

Challenge people about the change of life that comes when we believe in Jesus. We cannot believe in Jesus and keep on living as we did before. Jesus takes the place of whatever was at the centre of life. *Use your illustration.*

End

Give yourself to following Jesus. Make Jesus the centre of life.

Pray

Pray that you and every believer will have Jesus at the centre of your lives.

⬆ STUDY
WRONG HEART

Background

We have seen Jesus' followers start to spread the good news in Judea and Samaria. This passage continues the story of Philip in Samaria. Philip told people the good news. People turned from following a man called Simon and started following Jesus. This passage focuses on Simon. We see how he remains in his sin and needs to change.

Read

🎧 **READ** 8:14-25 two or three times.

Put each verse in your own words.

Understand

Read verses 14-17

- Why did the apostles in Jerusalem send Peter and John to Samaria?
- What is unusual about *when* the Holy Spirit comes on the new believers?

The strange thing here is that the Holy Spirit comes after people believe (v16-17). Some say this teaches that the gift of the Holy Spirit is a second step in the Christian life after believing in Jesus. But the normal pattern in Acts is that people receive the Holy Spirit when they believe (see Acts 2:38).

The rest of the New Testament tells us that every believer has the Holy Spirit (for example, Romans 8:9). So what happens here is unusual.

There is a good reason why the Holy Spirit was given later here. It was so the apostles from Jerusalem could see these were true believers. This is the first time people who are not Jews believe the good news about Jesus. People will question whether they are real believers. The apostles saw for themselves that they were.

🎧 **READ** verses 18-19

- How does Simon respond to what he sees?
- How does this fit with his previous life?

Simon wants to be able to give the Holy Spirit. He used to be the important person who everyone followed. Now Simon wants that importance again. He is willing to pay money to get this power.

🎧 **READ** verses 20-25

Verse 23: "Captive to sin" – held by the power of sin.

- What is wrong with Simon's attitude here?
- What does Peter say about Simon?
- What can we learn about Christian ministry?

The Holy Spirit is God's gift to all those who truly believe in Jesus. No one can buy God's free gift! Don't think you can control God.

Peter explains that Simon's heart is "not right before God" (v21). He is "full of bitterness and captive to sin" (v23). This might mean that he has not believed in Jesus. Or it could be that he has believed but his heart has not changed.

Sin is still at work in Simon. It controls how he is living. This may be because he is not born again, but believers can be caught in sin as well.

So Simon should now "repent of this wickedness" (v22). He must turn away from it and change. Simon's attitude means he has "no part or share in this ministry" (v21). Believers must not have wrong motives, such as a desire for power, selfishness, or pride. If our hearts are not right before God, we should not be involved in ministry or leading others.

Find the main point of the passage

Think about:

- What does this passage teach about heart attitudes?
- What is the main point of these verses?

The focus is on Simon and his wrong motives. Simon wants power, and he wants people to respect him. His heart is captive to sin. This means he can have no part in the work of Christian ministry.

The main point is about the bad motives people can have. They can have bad reasons for believing in Jesus. For example, they are only thinking of what they will get from it for themselves.

PLAN

Main point of the sermon

A sermon explains the passage, and applies it to your hearers. Look at the main point of the passage. Write what this main point will mean for your hearers.

It will be something like: We must never follow Jesus for what we can get.

Sub-points

- Read the main point again.
- Read the verses again.
- What sub-points will help you teach this passage?

The passage begins with the gift of the Holy Spirit. It then focuses on Simon's attitude and how sin controls him. Can you show this in your sub-points?

Think of a heading for each sub-point.

For example:

1. The problem: Wrong heart (v14-21, 23)

2. The answer: Turn back and ask for forgiveness (v22-25)

Illustrate

This passage shows someone who is "captive to sin" (v23). You can illustrate being held captive. A fly is held captive in a spider's web. It cannot break free. A prisoner is held captive by a locked door. He cannot get out. People are held captive by sin. It controls what they do. We need Jesus to release us so that we can be free.

Apply

Why do people want to believe in Jesus? Is it for what they think they will get out of it? Do they want power? Or money? Is it for how they think their life will get better?

Believers must be careful about wanting power or positions of authority. We must check our hearts and attitudes. We must turn away from selfish and wicked thoughts. We must be careful about our motives. Think carefully about how best to apply this to your people so that wrong attitudes are shown up.

Review

Check the main point is clear and that you keep to THIS passage.

 **TEACH**

Start

Talk about how God is concerned about our motives. People can do good things for bad reasons. This can mean people believe in Jesus for bad reasons. Or people serve in the church for bad reasons. This passage teaches us about this.

Explain

1. The problem: Wrong heart (v14-21, 23)

Explain why the gift of the Holy Spirit came later than usual for the Samarian Christians. This is not the main point so do not spend too much time on it. (Spend more time on this if people argue about the gift of the Holy Spirit in your place.)

Show how Simon wanted control of this gift of the Holy Spirit. Show how wrong his attitude was.

2. The answer: Turn back and ask for forgiveness (v22-25)

Simon must see what is wrong with himself (v23). He must repent (v22): Turn back to God and behave differently.

Call people to admit their sin and to turn from it. For people who are not believers this means turning to God for the first time. There may be believers who are trapped by a sin again and need to turn back to God.

Although Simon can be forgiven, he cannot have a part in Christian ministry. *Explain that the character of a person in Christian ministry is very important (v21).* Leaders do not need to be perfect, but they must not be captive to sin.

There may be specific ways to apply this in your place. Have Christian ministers been found guilty of sin? For example, sexual sin or financial sin. What doe people in the church think of this? What would Peter say?

Apply

Encourage people that there is an answer to being controlled by sin. We can turn to God and be forgiven. We can encourage each other in this and rejoice in forgiveness.

We must have church leaders who are good examples. Leaders must watch themselves carefully (see 1 Timothy 4:16).

End

Be careful not to believe in Jesus or serve Jesus in order to get things for yourself. If you do this, turn to God and ask for forgiveness.

Pray

Pray for God's help for those held captive by sin. Pray that your leaders will be good examples.

↑ STUDY
GOD'S MESSAGE SPREADS

Background

We have seen the message about Jesus spread in Jerusalem. Then persecution started. That meant the message about Jesus spread to Judea and Samaria. This is what Jesus said would happen (see Acts 1:8). God used Philip to spread the message in Samaria.

This passage continues to tell us about the work of Philip in spreading God's message. It also shows how God's message spreads to new types of people.

Read

↗ **READ** 8:26-40 two or three times.

Explain what happens in your own words.

Understand

↗ **READ** verses 26-28

Verse 27: "Eunuch" – a man who had had his private parts cut off. (Court officials were often eunuchs.)

Verse 28: "Chariot" – a cart pulled by horses to ride in.

- What important information are we given here?

An angel tells Philip to go to the road between Jerusalem and Gaza. This is the way home for the Ethiopian who came to Jerusalem to worship God. This man is important in the government of Ethiopia, in Africa. He may be a Jew, or a convert to Judaism. He believes enough to make a long journey to Jerusalem. Because he is a eunuch, he is not allowed into the inside courts of the temple (see Deuteronomy 23:1).

We have seen the good news about Jesus go to the Samaritans. Now it comes to someone else on the edge of the Jewish nation. Luke shows that the message about Jesus is spreading outside the Jews.

↗ **READ** verses 29-35

Verse 33: "Humiliation" – shame. "Deprived of" – not allowed.

- Which part of Scripture is the Ethiopian reading?
- What is the Ethiopian's question about the passage from Isaiah (v34)?
- How does Philip answer that question?
- Read all of Isaiah 53.

Philip is led by the Holy Spirit so he can talk to this person. Philip hears him reading and asks if he understands. The Ethiopian says he does not know what the passage from Isaiah is about. The passage is about someone suffering when they do not deserve it.

Philip explains that this passage from Isaiah is about Jesus. It tells us how Jesus suffered unjustly. But he suffered because of the sins of others. Jesus suffered for what his people did wrong. Jesus took the punishment for all his followers. See Isaiah 53:4-6, 10-11.

READ verses 36-40

- How does the Ethiopian respond to the message about Jesus?
- Why is Philip taken away?
- How does the Ethiopian feel?

The Ethiopian believes the good news of Jesus, and so he asks to be baptised. Baptism is a sign of his forgiveness and new life in Jesus.

Now that the Ethiopian has heard the good news about Jesus, Philip is not needed, so God takes him away to speak to people in other places. The Ethiopian goes home rejoicing. The message about Jesus is good news and it brings joy!

Find the main point of the passage

- What does this passage teach about God?
- What does it teach about the good news spreading to new people?

God leads Philip and tells him who to speak to, so this Ethiopian man comes to believe in Jesus. God wants people to know and understand the good news about Jesus. This man was from another country and was kept outside the temple. God now welcomes people who were kept outside before. God wants everyone to hear the good news.

For people to hear about Jesus, others need to tell them the good news. People like the Ethiopian need someone to teach them what the Bible means.

So the main point is that God wants new people to hear about Jesus. God uses people to explain the good news.

 **PLAN**

Main point of the sermon

A sermon explains the passage, and applies it to the hearers. Look at the main point of the passage. Write what this main point will mean for your hearers.

It will be something like: God wants new people to understand the good news about Jesus, and he uses his people to do this.

Sub-points

- Read the main point again.
- Read the verses again.
- What sub-points will help you teach this passage?

In this passage it is easier to teach main themes rather than break the passage into smaller parts.

For example:

1. God wants people to understand the good news

2. God wants to use his people to explain the good news

Illustrate

If you have an important message, you will make sure people hear about it. Imagine you know where water is in a drought. You will tell people. You will ask all your friends to pass the message on. You will make sure people understand the message and what it means.

God worked in Jesus to bring forgiveness. God wants everyone to hear that message and understand it fully.

Apply

God wants people to understand the message of the good news about Jesus. We can apply this differently to two groups of people. Some people will not understand or believe the message. So ask people if they have understood the message about Jesus. Explain the good news from Isaiah 53—how Jesus died in the place of those who turn to him.

Then apply the passage to those who do understand and believe. God wants them to tell other people and explain the good news.

Review

Check the main point is clear and that you keep to THIS passage.

 **TEACH**

Start

You could start with your illustration.

You may start by talking about what God has done in Jesus. What does God want to happen next? He wants everyone to hear and to understand the good news. This passage is about how God works for one person to understand about Jesus.

Explain

Introduction

Remind people who Philip is and what he has done. Now God directs Philip to a specific road. God has a job for him to do.

1. God wants people to understand the good news

God wants the Ethiopian eunuch to understand the good news. God arranges for Phillip to meet him, and for the Ethiopian to be reading Isaiah 53 when they meet!

The Ethiopian does not understand what he is reading. Philip explains that it is about Jesus dying for his people. Jesus takes the punishment so his people can go free. This is what God wants the Ethiopian to understand. The Ethiopian does understand and believes. He shows this by being baptised.

2. God wants to use his people to explain the good news

God uses others to help people understand the message of Jesus. That is why Philip meets the Ethiopian and talks to him. The Ethiopian needed to be taught from the Bible. God wants people who understand the good news about Jesus' death to explain it to others.

Apply

Do we read the Bible but not really know what it means? *Apply this to people who are not believers. They need to hear the Bible explained so they understand about Jesus. Explain why Jesus died, and ask them if they understand and believe—like the Ethiopian did.*

Encourage believers to explain the good news to others. Lots of people will know something about Jesus or read the Bible, but not understand properly. We need to explain the truth to them so they can believe. God wants to use us.

End

God wants everyone to hear and understand the good news about Jesus. God uses us to spread this wonderful message.

Pray

Pray your church will understand the good news and explain it to others.

⬆ STUDY
THE GREAT CHANGE

Background

We have seen the good news about Jesus spread from Jerusalem as people scattered because of persecution. Luke told us about someone involved in that persecution: Saul. Look at chapter 8:1-3.

This passage is about Saul. Saul will be very significant in the life of the church. Saul is the man who becomes the apostle "Paul". So far we saw him persecuting the church. Now God turns him around.

Read

READ verses 9:1-31 two or three times.

For each few verses say what happens in your own words.

Understand

READ verses 1-2

Verse 2: "Synagogues" – places where Jews met for teaching and prayer.

Verse 2: "Damascus" – the capital of Syria, north east from Jerusalem.

- What is Saul's attitude to Christian believers?

Saul wants to destroy the church. He put believers in prison in Jerusalem.

Now he wants to do the same in Damascus. Saul is completely against Jesus and people who believe in Jesus.

READ verses 3-9

Verse 7: "Speechless" – had no words.

- Explain what happens to Saul in your own words.
- Why does Jesus say Saul is persecuting him (Jesus)?
- What will this teach Saul?

Jesus appears to Saul in a bright light and speaks to him. The men with Saul do not see anyone. When Saul gets up, he is blind and needs other people to lead him. He does not eat or drink for three days.

Jesus asks Saul why he is persecuting him. This is because Jesus is connected with people who believe in him. They are like his "body". So what happens to the believers also happens to Jesus.

Saul is forced to realise that Jesus is alive. This means the message about Jesus is true. Saul thought it was dangerous lies. But now Saul accepts he was very wrong.

READ verses 10-19

Verse 15: "Gentiles" – people who are not Jews.

- How does Ananias feel about God's instructions?
- What does God explain?
- What does God say Saul will do (v15)?

Ananias does not want to see Saul. Ananias knows Saul came to Damascus to arrest people like him! But God tells Ananias he has a plan for Saul's life. God will use Saul to spread the message about Jesus. So Ananias obeys and goes to Saul. Notice his first words to him: "Brother Saul". Although he knows all Saul has done, Ananias now sees him as a brother because Saul trusts in Jesus.

READ verses 20-31

Verse 21: "Caused havoc" – brought distress and fear.

Verse 22: "Baffled" – could not answer him.

- What does Saul start to do?
- What same event happens in Damascus and then in Jerusalem?

Saul begins to preach the truth about Jesus. Saul tells people that Jesus is the Messiah promised in the Old Testament. In both Damascus and Jerusalem the believers are not sure if they can trust Saul, but then they do. In both places Saul is opposed. There is a plan to kill him but he escapes. Saul has changed from being the person persecuting Christian believers to being persecuted himself!

Find the main point of the passage

- What does this passage tell us about God?
- What does this passage tell us about opposition to Jesus?
- What does this passage tell us about who God uses?

We see how God takes the person most against Jesus and turns him around. God makes Saul a great preacher about Jesus. This shows God can change anyone. It shows no opposition to Jesus is too big for God to overcome.

So the main point is that God's plans to spread the good news can never be stopped.

PLAN

Main point of the sermon

Your sermon will explain the passage, and apply it to your hearers. Look at the main point of the passage. Write what this main point will mean for your hearers.

It will be something like: God's plans for the good news to spread will never be stopped, because he is stronger than any opposition.

Sub-points

- Read the main point again.
- Read the verses again.
- What sub-points will help you teach this passage?

In this passage it is best to go through what happens and then bring out the main lessons.

For example:

1. Saul opposes Jesus (v1-2)

2. Jesus appears to Saul (v3-19)

3. Saul proclaims Jesus (v20-31)

Illustrate

This passage is about someone changing direction completely. You may talk about someone who changes sides in a fight and then fights for the people he was fighting against. Why would someone do that? Because he realised he was fighting on the wrong side. But what happens when he does that? The people he was with before now fight against him. This is what happened to Saul.

You may be able to tell the story of someone you know who was turned around by God and is now preaching for Jesus.

Apply

God wants the good news about Jesus to spread to everyone. God can take the person most against Jesus and make him someone who spreads that message.

Can you think of someone who is strongly against Jesus? Do you think that person is too hard for God to change? Pray the light of Jesus will shine into their life. Think of those who persecute Christians today—in your country or other countries in the world. Pray for them.

Review

Check the main point is clear and that you keep to THIS passage.

 **TEACH**

Start

Begin by speaking about opposition that believers face in your situation. There may be people who fight against the good news about Jesus and against God's people. That was how it was for Christians in Acts. The man called Saul led the persecution.

Explain

1. Saul opposes Jesus (v1-2)

Remind people who Saul is. Show how Saul tried to destroy the church, from 8:1-3 and 9:1-2. Saul was completely against Jesus and everyone who believed in Jesus. Saul thought the message about Jesus was a lie and must be stopped. *Show how people oppose Jesus in your place.*

2. Jesus appears to Saul (v3-19)

Explain what happens. Jesus shows Saul that he is alive and in control. Jesus says that Saul is persecuting him. Saul realised he was wrong. God has big plans for Saul. God will use Saul to spread the message about Jesus to those who are not Jews (Gentiles).

3. Saul proclaims Jesus (v20-31)

Saul starts to preach that Jesus is the Son of God. He proves this is true from the Old Testament. *Show what a complete change this is. Use your illustration.* Saul has changed sides! He now fights for the side he was fighting against.

This means people are now against Saul. People plot against him in Damascus, and again in Jerusalem. The believers help him escape.

Apply

God turned around someone who hated Jesus. God made him a great preacher about Jesus. *Think how this best applies to your people.*

No opposition is too big for God. Remember, God can turn people who are against believers and make them preachers about Jesus. Do we believe God can do this? Do we believe God can change the hardest people into great evangelists who tell others about Jesus? That is what God did with Saul. We should trust God and pray he will change persecutors we know.

End

God takes the biggest enemy of Jesus and his followers, and turns him around. Be confident in God and the spread of his message.

Pray

Pray for those you know who are persecuted, and for those who persecute them.

⬆ STUDY
POINT TO JESUS

Background

We have seen the good news about Jesus spreading. After spreading in Jerusalem it spread in Judea and Samaria. Saul persecuted the church. Then God turned Saul around. Now Saul preaches about Jesus.

In this passage we return to the apostle Peter. We last saw Peter with John in chapter 8, visiting the new church in Samaria. Peter travels round the country visiting believers and preaching the good news.

Read

🕗 **READ** 9:32-43 two or three times in different translations if you can.

Put each verse in your own words.

Understand

🕗 **READ** verses 32-35

Verse 32: "Holy people" (or "saints" in some translations) – people who believe in Jesus and so are "holy" because of what Jesus did for them.

Verse 33: "Bedridden" – cannot get out of bed.

- What details are given about Aeneas?
- Does what Peter says remind you of Jesus?

- What is the result of this healing?

Peter visits the believers in Lydda and one man is ill. He has not left his bed for eight years. Peter tells him that Jesus heals him and he must get up and roll up his mat. This is very like what Jesus said to a paralysed man in Luke 5:24. The result is that many people turn to the Lord. They repent and believe in Jesus.

🕗 **READ** verses 36-43

Verse 36, 38: "Disciple" – someone who believes in Jesus and follow him.

- What details are we told about Tabitha?
- Why do the disciples send for Peter?
- What does Peter do that reminds you of Jesus?
- What does this tell us about how God uses miracles?

Tabitha/Dorcas did many good actions and helped the poor. She made clothes for people. She is a good example. Peter is called to see if he can raise Tabitha from the dead. The believers do not try to raise Tabitha themselves—they know they need Peter. In the same way Aeneas is not healed by the believers in Lydda. We saw in other studies that Jesus gave his apostles the power to heal in a special way. That is why it is Peter who does these miracles.

Peter sends people out of the room, prays and tells Tabitha to get up. This is very like what Jesus did with a young girl in Luke 8:51-56. The result is exactly the same in Lydda. Many people believe in Jesus.

Peter does two amazing miracles. This shows the power of Jesus at work. In Acts 3 Peter told the crowd that healings show that Jesus is exalted as God's Messiah (3:12-16). We see the same here.

The focus is on Peter: He is a representative of Jesus. Peter does two miracles that are very like miracles of Jesus. So Jesus continues his work through Peter. This shows how important the apostles are.

Find the main point of the passage

- What does this tell about Jesus?
- What is the focus of this passage?

Jesus is at work through his apostles. They have special power to heal. The result is not only that people are amazed at the healing. People believe in Jesus. Miracles point people to Jesus to believe

in him. (You may want to read the "extra" section on miracles on p. 52.)

God may still heal today, but he worked differently through his apostles. If God does heal today, he wants people to see that Jesus is at work and to believe in him.

The main point will be something like: The miracles of the apostles point people to Jesus so that they believe in him.

⬇ PLAN

Main point of the sermon

Write your main point…

The miracles of the apostles point people to Jesus.

Sub-points

This passage is best taken as one unit. You can tell the whole story and then make the points from it.

- Read the main point again.
- Read the verses again.
- What sub-points will help you teach this passage?

The miracles point to who Jesus is— so you should call people to realise who Jesus is. The miracles show the importance of Jesus' apostles. (These are the 13 original apostles, not people called apostles today.) The overall message is that people believe in Jesus. That comes from realising who Jesus is and trusting the message of the apostles. So we can call people to respond to the offer of forgiveness through belief in Jesus. So the sub-points could be these:

1. Realise who Jesus is (v32-34, 36-41)

2. Respond to Jesus' offer of forgiveness (v35, 42)

Illustrate

Some people have identity (ID) cards which prove who they are. These cards may show they have authority—like the police. Or it may show they have a special skill—like a doctor. These people can prove who they are and what role they have. God gave his 13 apostles the ability to heal to prove who they were. Miracles showed the special identity of the apostles like Peter and then pointed people to Jesus.

Apply

How you apply will depend on your situation. If people run after miracles and "healers", you will want to talk more about how miracles must always point to Jesus. Miracles today do not prove the authority of the person. Jesus said there will be many false teachers who perform miracles (Matthew 7:21-23). Many miracles today focus on the healer and not on Jesus. Warn people about this.

Review

Check the main point is clear and you keep to THIS passage.

TEACH

Start

This passage is about miracles which point to Jesus. How you begin depends on what people think of miracles in your situation. Are people disappointed if God does not do miracles? Or people may not believe in miracles. This passage will help us understand more.

Explain

Explain the story first and then bring lessons from it. Point out details about Aeneas and Tabitha. Show how Peter heals immediately and completely.

Show that Peter does not have power to do this himself. He depends on Jesus. He says to Aeneas: "Jesus Christ heals you" (v34), and he prays on his knees for Tabitha (v40). Show how both healings end. Notice people do not ask for more healings. They turn to trust in Jesus for salvation. That is more important than physical healing.

1. Realise who Jesus is (v32-34, 36-41)

The message about Jesus is spreading. More and more people trust in Jesus.

Explain Jesus gave his apostles the ability to heal. Miracles show these men are Jesus' "apostles", sent to speak about him. This is why the believers send for Peter: Aeneas is only healed when Peter arrives.

So we must not expect people today to perform miracles like Peter. We can pray for healing. But we do not expect it in the same way. God may heal today; he may not. He has not promised to heal through us.

Jesus shows who he is by miracles through the apostles. These miracles done in Jesus' name are like the miracles Jesus did (Luke 5:24, 8:51). They show Jesus is alive and active.

Ask people who they think Jesus is. Do they understand he is God's Saviour, now reigning in heaven?

2. Respond to Jesus' offer of forgiveness (v35, 42)

The miracles point to Jesus. People respond by trusting Jesus.

Ask your hearers if they have trusted in Jesus. Explain that means knowing who Jesus is, and how he rescues people from their sin. It means turning to Jesus (v35) and believing in him (v42).

Apply

Look back to PLAN.

End

The miracles the 13 apostles did point us to trust in Jesus.

Pray

Pray that you will be focused on Jesus and knowing him.

⬆ STUDY
THE GOOD NEWS IS FOR EVERYONE

Background

So far the good news about Jesus has been taught to the Jews (chapters 2 – 7) and then to the Samaritans (chapter 8). Now Peter is challenged to take God's message to the Gentiles (those who are not Jews). God teaches Peter that the good news is for everyone. This is shocking for the Jews! The Jews thought God belonged to them— that they alone were the people of God.

Read

🎧 **READ** 10:1-43 out loud.

Use your own words to explain what happens in each paragraph.

Understand

🎧 **READ** verses 1-8

Verse 1: "Centurion" – a commander in the Roman army.

Verse 2: "God-fearing" – someone who worships the God of the Jews but has not fully converted to Judaism.

Verse 4: "Memorial offering" – a sacrifice in the Old Testament.

- What are we told about Cornelius?
- What would the Jews think of Cornelius, a Roman?
- What does the angel say to Cornelius?

Cornelius is a Gentile who does worship the true God. But he has not converted fully to Judaism. Jews think he is "unclean" or spiritually dirty. There was hatred between Jews and Gentiles. Jews never went into a Gentile's house or ate with them.

The angel says the prayers and gifts of Cornelius came as an offering to God. God was happy with them. Cornelius is given instructions to bring Peter from Joppa.

🎧 **READ** verses 9-23

Verse 10: "Trance" – as if he was dreaming.

Verse 14: "Impure" or "unclean" – spiritually dirty animals that Jews were not allowed to eat.

- What does the voice in the vision tell Peter?
- Why does the vision happen at the same time as the men sent by Cornelius arrive?
- What is the purpose of the vision?

Peter sees a vision of animals. This includes some animals thought to be "clean" and some "unclean". The voice tells Peter he must not call anything God has made impure or unclean. God is teaching Peter the rules about eating certain foods in the Old Testament are only a picture.

The men from Cornelius arrive at the same time because Peter also thinks Gentiles are unclean. God's vision to Peter is a lesson about the Gentiles.

READ verses 24-43

Verse 25: "Reverence" – respect.

Verse 29: "Raising an objection" – reasons to say no.

Verse 34: "Favouritism" – unfairly treat some people as better than others.

- What does Peter say God taught him?
- What does Cornelius expect Peter to do?
- What does Peter now understand?
- What does Peter then do in verses 36-43?

Peter says the law stopped him from going to a Gentile's house. But God's vision taught him not to call any person impure or unclean.

But Peter does not know why he is there. Cornelius tells him they are ready to listen to what God commands Peter to tell them.

Peter realises he is meant to tell the message about Jesus to everyone— Jews and Gentiles. Peter sees God does not put one person above another but will accept anyone who responds to him.

So Peter tells Gentiles the good news of how sins are forgiven by believing in Jesus.

Find the main point of the passage

- What does this passage tell us about how God thinks of different groups of people?
- What does this passage tell about who God wants to hear the good news of Jesus?

God organises a meeting between Peter, a Jew, and Cornelius, a Gentile. God does this so that Cornelius and other Gentiles can hear the good news about Jesus. God wants the good news to go to everyone, whatever the differences between them.

So the main point is that God wants everyone to hear the good news.

93

PLAN

Main point of the sermon

Your sermon will explain the passage, and apply the passage to your hearers. Look at the main point of the passage. Write what this main point will mean for your hearers.

The good news about Jesus is for everyone.

Sub-points

- Read the main point again.
- Read the verses again.
- What sub-points will help you teach this passage?

The main point is that the good news is for everyone. Everyone must hear about Jesus, even if there are cultural barriers. (A barrier is a block. It is something that stops friendship.) Your sub-points can follow the passage in making these points.

The sub points may be:

1. There are barriers between people (v1-23)

2. The good news must cross all barriers (v24-43)

Illustrate

Tell a story of how people crossed cultural or social barriers to tell the good news of Jesus. Tell a story of people who were against each other, and how they were united by the good news of Jesus. This may be a story you know from your situation. Or it may be a story from elsewhere.

Apply

We must tell the good news of Jesus to everyone. We must do this whatever differences there are between us. Differences of race, tribe or anything else must not stop the spread of the good news.

Think what differences may get in the way of spreading the good news in your situation.

Review

Check the main point is clear and that you keep to THIS passage.

 **TEACH**

Start

Think of groups of people in your place who do not like each other. Or groups who are separated. That may be different tribes, or different groups in the community. The good news of Jesus is for all these different groups.

Explain

1. There are barriers between people (v1-23)

Explain the background of how Jews and Gentiles lived apart. There was a huge barrier between them. This meant the good news of Jesus didn't go to the Gentiles. God wanted to change this.

Explain the background of unclean animals. Point out Peter's strong response. Show how God is teaching Peter not to call things unclean. Explain that even when Peter goes to meet Cornelius he does not understand what he is to do. The barriers between Jews and Gentiles were very strong. They kept these two groups separate. That meant the good news about Jesus did not spread to the Gentiles.

2. The good news must cross all barriers (v24-43)

God teaches Peter that he must not think of Gentiles as unclean. Peter must not think Gentiles are outside God's plan. *Focus on the key verses which show what Peter learns.* Verse 28 says God taught Peter not to think of people as impure or unclean. Verse 34 shows he learned that God does not think more of one person than another.

Show people how Peter finally understands that the gospel is for everyone. God does not have favourite people. So Peter tells Cornelius and others the good news about Jesus. Peter tells them that "everyone" who believes in Jesus will be forgiven (verse 43).

Apply

Are there people we don't speak to about Jesus? Are there tribes or groups of people we ignore or hate? Are there barriers that separate us from others? God calls us to not have favourite people. We must speak the good news to everyone.

End

God wants everyone to hear the good news.

Pray

Pray that you and your hearers will spread the good news about Jesus to everyone. Pray you will cross barriers with the good news of Jesus.

↑ STUDY
ONE IN JESUS

Background

The good news about Jesus spread to Jews (chapters 2 – 7) and then to Samaritans (chapter 8).

Now God has taught Peter that the good news must go to Gentiles (chapter 10). God said never to think of some people as unclean. Don't think that the good news is not for them. Peter understood that God does not have favourite people. God wants the good news of Jesus to go to everyone.

This passage continues the story of Peter meeting with Cornelius and his household. It shows the results of that meeting and how Jews and Gentiles become one in Jesus.

Read

READ 10:44 – 11:18 two or three times.

In your own words explain what happens in each few verses.

Understand

READ 10:44-48

Verse 45: "Circumcised believers" – Jewish believers.

- What happens while Peter is explaining the good news?
- How does God show that Cornelius and the others are true believers?
- Why are the "circumcised believers" who came with Peter so surprised?
- What does Peter conclude from what happened?

God gives the gift of the Holy Spirit as he did at Pentecost (chapter 2). This is shown by speaking in tongues. This means Peter and others see that the Gentiles receive the Spirit as they did. This is how God shows him that Cornelius and the others are true believers.

The Jewish believers who came with Peter are "astonished" (v45). This is because they still thought the Gentiles were different. They did not think God would treat them the same way as Jews. They thought the gift of the Holy Spirit was only for Jews.

Peter understands that the Gentiles who believed are equal believers. This means they should be baptised. Look at the way Peter says this in verse 47. No one can stand in the way of their baptism. God has made it clear they are equal believers. To stop them being baptised would be to go against God.

READ 11:1-18

Verse 2: "Uncircumcised believers" – believers who are Gentiles / non-Jews.

- What concerns do the Jewish believers have?
- How does Peter answer them?
- What is their conclusion?

The Jewish believers think Peter did something wrong—he went to a Gentile's house and ate with them! They think Peter has broken the law. They still think Jews and Gentiles are different, and they can't be friends.

Peter explains everything that happened. He repeats the story from chapter 10 because it is so important. The Jewish believers must understand that God was in this. This teaches them that God wanted Peter to go to Cornelius and tell him and his household the message about Jesus.

Notice Peter's words in verse 17. God gave the Gentile believers the same gift that he gave the Jewish believers. Because God did that, then they must not stand in God's way. They must see what God is doing and go along with God's plan.

The Jewish believers in Jerusalem listen to Peter. They see that God is in this. They have no more concerns, and they praise God for giving the Gentiles repentance and new life in Jesus. Look at 1 Corinthians 12:12-13. These are important verses, which show the unity of all believers.

Find the main point of the passage

- What does this teach us about accepting people who believe in Jesus?
- What does it show about unity (oneness) in the church?
- Why is this passage included in Acts?

This passage shows that everyone who believes in Jesus is equal. This teaches that believers all receive the same Holy Spirit. There are no "second-class" believers.

The main point is that all believers are equal and united in Jesus.

97

PLAN

Main point of the sermon

Your sermon will explain the passage, and apply the passage to your hearers. Look at the main point of the passage. Write what this main point will mean for your hearers.

It will be something like this: All believers are equal and are made one in Jesus.

Sub-points

- Read the main point again.
- Read the verses again.
- What sub-points will help you teach this passage?

Look at what is different from 10:44-48 and 11:1-18. The first part shows God's action. The second part then shows people's acceptance. This can shape your sub points.

The sub points may be:

1. Confirming people as true believers (10:44-48)

2. Accepting people as true believers (11:1-18)

Illustrate

Can you tell a story of how people have been made one in Jesus? Maybe people from different tribes or countries. People who do not like each other, or even hate each other. For example, people in China often hate people from Japan because of past wars. But Chinese believers are united with Japanese believers.

Apply

We must treat anyone who believes in Jesus as equal. We must be united by Jesus. That affects how we think about other believers. We must not think some believers are better than others. We must not think some believers are more important than others. We must not think some believers are more deserving than others.

This will change how we behave to others. We will welcome and love all believers. We will not have favourites. We will live out the unity that Jesus brings.

Review

Check the main point is clear and that you keep to THIS passage.

 **TEACH**

Start

People can be separated by race, tribe, age or sex. It can be because of history: For example, wars between people. Sin separates us from God and from each other. God sent Jesus to make people right with him. God also sent Jesus so we can be united to other believers. That is what this passage teaches.

Explain

1. Confirming people as true believers (10:44-48)

God gives the Gentiles the sign of speaking in other languages. This shows the Jewish believers that these Gentiles have received the Holy Spirit.

The Jewish believers with Peter are "astonished" (v45). They did not think the Gentiles could be equal with Jewish believers. *Explain Peter's words in verse 47.* The Gentiles received God's Spirit in the same way as the Jews. That means they should be baptised.

This confirms the Gentile believers are true believers and equal with the Jews. No believers are more important or special than others.

2. Accepting people as true believers (11:1-18)

The Jewish believers in Jerusalem thought Peter did something wrong. This is because of their view of Gentiles. Peter tells them the whole story so they can see how this was from God.

Explain Peter's words in verse 17. The Jewish and Gentile believers received the "same gift" as each other—the Holy Spirit (see 10:47). If anyone is against the Gentiles being welcomed as equal believers, then they are against God.

The Jewish believers understand and praise God for including the Gentiles. Look at 1 Corinthians 12:12-13. Whatever differences which separate people (being Gentile or Jew; being slave or free), believers are now united as one body in Jesus. *Use your illustration.*

Apply

God has united everyone who believes in Jesus. All believers are equal, whatever their background. Our attitude to people must be different. We must change how we live as God's people. *Give some practical examples of this.*

End

God gives the same gift of the Holy Spirit to all believers, so we are all made one in Jesus.

Pray

Pray that your church will live out this oneness in Christ.

⬆ STUDY
WHAT GOD WANTS TO SEE

Background

We have seen in chapters 10 and 11 that God wants everyone to hear the good news, and the good news unites everyone. Luke writes this passage to show these truths in action.

Read

READ 11:19-30 two or three times.

Say the meaning of each sentence in your own words.

Understand

READ verses 19-21

- What do the believers who were scattered do?
- What are the differences in who they speak to?
- How does this connect to Peter's experience in chapters 10 – 11?

God taught Peter that the good news is for everyone, including Gentiles (chapter 10). Now Luke tells us about the spread of the message to more people who are not Jews. Some believers speak only to Jews (v19). Maybe they think Jesus is the Saviour only for Jews. Or maybe they were afraid to speak to Gentiles. But the second group of believers speak to Greeks as well, and tell them about Jesus.

The message is spread among Greeks in Antioch (a city north of Jerusalem in what is now Turkey). Jesus is at work and many people believe and turn to Jesus (v21). What a wonderful picture!

READ verses 22-26

- Why does the church in Jerusalem send Barnabas to Antioch?
- Why is Barnabas so glad at what he sees?
- Why does he bring Saul to help?

The church in Jerusalem want to know what is happening in Antioch and help them. Barnabas is glad because he saw signs of the grace of God (v23). This may be people turning from their sin, asking for forgiveness, living to please God, loving each other, and telling people about Jesus. These are things that show God is at work.

Barnabas helps strengthen the new believers. He encourages them to remain faithful to Jesus (v23). He brings Saul to help teach this new church. This gave a good opportunity for Saul, but Barnabas probably also needed help.

Teachers are needed to strengthen believers.

This was the first church that was a mixture of Jews and Gentiles. So they could not be thought of as part of Judaism. They needed a new name. "Christian" (v26) means someone who belongs to Christ and follows him.

READ verses 27-30

Verse 28: "Predicted" – told before it happened.

Verse 28: "Roman world" – the area ruled by the Romans.

- Why do the disciples send a gift to the believers in Jerusalem?
- What relationship do they feel with believers in Jerusalem (v29)?
- Why is this a wonderful picture of Christian love?

A famine in the Roman world is predicted. The believers in Antioch collect money to help care for believers in Judea. This is a lovely picture of Christian love. They think of the believers in Judea as "brothers and sisters" (v29). They do not know them personally and the believers in Judea were Jews. This is a wonderful example of how believers in Jesus are united.

Find the main point of the passage

- What does this passage tell us about how Jesus wants his message to spread?
- What does it tell us about the life of a local church?
- What does it tell us about caring for other believers?

This passage is a picture of what God wants to see in his people. God wants people to tell the good news of Jesus, especially to new groups of people. God wants people to stand strong in the truth of the good news about Jesus and so live for him. This is why we need teachers. God wants his people united and loving each other. This shows itself in practical care and support.

So God wants the good news to spread and change how people live.

PLAN

Main point of the sermon

A sermon explains the passage, and applies the passage to the hearers. Look at the main point of the passage. Write what this main point will mean for your hearers.

God wants the good news to spread to new people and change the way they live.

Sub-points

- Read the main point again.
- Read the verses again.
- What sub-points will help you teach this passage?

In the study we saw there are three parts to this passage. The good news spread to new people. Then those people needed teaching. Then those people showed care for other believers. Use these three parts for your sub-points.

The sub points may be:

1. God wants new people to hear the good news (v19-21)

2. God wants people to be taught the good news (v22-26)

3. God wants people to be united by the good news (v27-30)

Illustrate

Tell a story of how the good news of Jesus changed someone's life. How they went from living as boss of their life to having God in control. How their priorities changed. How their relationships changed. How they started to care about other Christians. This is the difference the good news about Jesus makes. It changes lives. This is what we see in this passage. This is what God wants to see in our churches.

Apply

You can apply each of the three sub-points separately.

- How can we tell the good news of Jesus to more people? What people can we reach who have not heard about Jesus?
- How can we be strong and grow up in our faith through good teaching? How can we teach and encourage others?
- How can we be united and caring as a church?

Think of specific examples for each of these.

Review

Check the main point is clear and that you keep to THIS passage.

 # TEACH

Start

Ask what God wants from a church. What are God's priorities? This passage gives an example of what God wants. It gives a picture of a model church—a church doing well.

Explain

1. God wants new people to hear the good news (v19-21)

Explain how people were spread by persecution (8:1). Remind people of the big barrier: Hatred between Jews and Gentiles at that time. This means some believers will only speak to Jews. Others speak to Greeks as well. God is with this second group of believers, and through them he brings many more people to trust in Jesus.

Apply this by asking if there are groups we do not speak the good news to. Are there some people we do not reach out to? We must speak to everyone about Jesus.

2. God wants people to be taught the good news (v22-26)

Barnabas comes to the church in Antioch. He is glad at what he sees. He encourages people to stay faithful. He gets Saul to help him teach the church, so that people understand the good news better. Once we believe the good news, God wants us to understand it better. So we need teachers.

Apply this by encouraging people to keep learning. Also encourage people to be involved in teaching and encouraging each other.

3. God wants people to be united by the good news (v27-30)

A hungry time is coming. The believers in Antioch want to help the believers in Judea. This passage shows different people united by Jesus. Believing in Jesus makes us brothers and sisters with each other.

Apply this by encouraging people to care for other believers like a family. Give examples of care in your church. Give examples of care to believers in another church that may be very different from yours.

Apply

Each point has already been applied. Which is the most important one for your situation? Use your illustration.

End

God wants to see the good news about Jesus spreading to new people, changing people and uniting his church.

Pray

Pray that your church will spread the good news, grow and be united.

⬆ STUDY
21 HEROD AGAINST GOD

Background

This passage finishes another main section of Acts. In the first section (chapters 1 – 6) we saw the good news spread in Jerusalem among Jews. In the second section we see the start of persecution and the spread of the good news to new people groups (chapters 8 – 11).

The section ends by returning to Jerusalem and the persecution of believers there.

Read

READ 12:1-25 two or three times.

Say the meaning of each sentence in your own words.

Understand

READ verses 1-5

Verse 3: "Seize" – arrest.

Verse 3: "Festival of Unleavened Bread" – part of the Passover festival, remembering rescue from Egypt.

- Why does King Herod persecute the church leaders?
- What is Peter's situation (v4)?
- What two sides of a spiritual fight are seen in verse 5?

King Herod arrests some of the believers and James is killed. Herod continues because he sees the Jews are pleased. Peter is arrested and kept under strong guard. Peter escaped from prison earlier (5:19). Herod does not want this to happen again. Peter will probably be killed like James.

Verse 5 shows the fight. Peter is in prison under guard. But the church is praying for him. It is a fight between the power of King Herod and the power of prayer.

READ verses 6-17

Verse 11: "Clutches" – grasp.

Verse 12: "Dawned on him" – he realised it.

- Explain what happens.
- Did Peter realise what was happening (v9, 11, 12)?
- How do the believers respond when Peter arrives?

God sends an angel to free Peter. Peter does not know what is happening. It is only later (v11) that he suddenly sees he is rescued from Herod.

The believers are praying for Peter. But when he arrives, they do not realise it is really him! They say it must be his messenger (the word for angel also means messenger, v15). Then they realise what God has done. Luke shows this clearly. Neither Peter nor the believers realised what God was doing.

This makes us ask: Do we believe in the power of prayer?

READ verses 18-25

Verse 18: "No small commotion" – big confusion.

- How does Herod respond to Peter's escape?
- What is Herod's attitude when he is praised?
- What is the difference between how the passage begins and how it ends?

Herod is very angry at Peter's escape. Herod is made to look stupid. Luke then writes about an event in Caesarea. The people from Tyre and Sidon need Herod's help to get food. So they speak about him as a "god" (v22). Herod accepts the praise. So God sends another angel. This time the angel comes to kill.

The passage began with Herod killing James; it ends with God killing Herod. This shows going against God will never work. God will always win.

Find the main point of the passage

- What does this passage tell us about opposition to believers?
- What does it tell us about prayer?

The main point of this passage is that God is more powerful than Herod. That means prayer to God is more powerful than Herod's guards and prison. It also means Herod will be judged for his pride.

Note:

Be careful how you preach this. People could get wrong expectations. This passage shows how God rescues Peter in a miraculous way. But we must also remember that James was killed. The believers probably prayed for him as well as for Peter, but God allowed James to die. Many people who persecute Christians are not killed as Herod was. So we need to teach these points carefully, and say that we do not know what God will do in any situation.

 **PLAN**

Main point of the sermon

The sermon explains the passage, and applies the passage to the hearers. Look at the main point of the passage. Write what this main point will mean for your hearers.

It will be something like: God is more powerful than anyone else. So in times of opposition we must pray to God and trust God will win in the end.

Sub-points

- Read the main point again.
- Read the verses again.
- What sub-points will help you teach this passage?

Look through the flow of the passage. How can you divide it up? What points do you want to make about prayer and about God judging people?

The sub points may be:

1. Expect persecution—it is normal for believers (v1-4)

2. Pray to God—he is powerful (v5-17)

3. Look ahead—God will win (v18-25)

Illustrate

Think of a story of how God answered prayer in a surprising way which goes with the main point of this passage. Or stories of how people trusted God during persecution and prayed to him.

Apply

Think how your people most need this passage applied to them. If you are being persecuted, use it to encourage—remembering God does not always deliver his people as he did Peter.

Or think of examples of when we do not really expect God to answer prayer. Think how you could challenge your people to pray more, expecting God to answer. Challenge people to think about who they truly believe is more powerful—God, or people who are opposing them. That may be the government or other religious leaders.

Review

Check the main point is clear and that you keep to THIS passage.

 **TEACH**

Start

Mention ways believers face opposition in your place. That may be physical harm, fines, or being ignored and laughed at.

Explain

1. Expect persecution—it is normal for believers (v1-4)

There has been persecution before (Acts 4:2-3; 8:1). Now it looks more powerful. King Herod arrests believers and kills James. Herod wants to be popular with the Jews and so he arrests Peter too. The situation is bad. Peter is under strong guard. He will probably be killed.

Opposition is normal. We can expect it. We see it through Acts (and in history). Sometimes believers have times of peace, but often they are persecuted. Sometimes that includes persecution from the governing authorities.

2. Pray to God—he is powerful (v5-17)

Show this is like a fight between Herod and the people praying. Herod looks very strong. Prayer looks weak. But God is powerful and God answers prayer.

Explains the details of the escape (v6-11) and how Peter does not realise what is happening. Peter only understands when he is free. The same thing happens with the believers who are praying. They do not believe Peter is free. Luke writes like this to challenge us: Do we believe in the power of prayer? Do we pray expecting God to answer?

3. Look ahead—God will win (v18-25)

Explain the details of the meeting with people from Tyre and Sidon. Show Herod's attitude of pride. The true God then punishes him for this. The passage ends every differently to how it began. Rather than Herod killing believers, God kills Herod.

God does not kill leaders every time they oppose his people. This is not usual. But we learn God is more powerful. He will judge those who oppose him.

Apply

How do you respond if you are persecuted for following Jesus? This passage tells us not to be surprised. It tells us to pray, and trust God to work. It tells us to remember God will win. *Use your illustration.*

End

God is more powerful than any human government. Pray and trust God when you are persecuted.

Pray

Think how your people most need to change in response to this message and pray for that.

⬆ STUDY
THE GOOD NEWS SPREADS OUT

Background

The plan for the book of Acts is in Jesus' words in Acts 1:8: "You will be my witnesses in Jerusalem, and in all Judea and Samaria, and to the ends of the earth". We have seen the good news about Jesus spread in Jerusalem, and then in Judea and Samaria.

The book of Acts is in six big sections. We have seen the first three (1:1 – 6:7; 6:8 – 9:31; 9:32 – 12:24). We now see a new section which continues until 16:5. This is the start of being witnesses "to the ends of the earth". The focus is on the apostle Paul. He makes a number of "missionary journeys", where he takes the good news about Jesus to new places.

This map below shows the first journey Paul and Barnabas take. This covers chapters 13 – 14.

Read

READ verses 13:1-12 two or three times.

Explain each verse in your own words.

Understand

READ verses 1-3

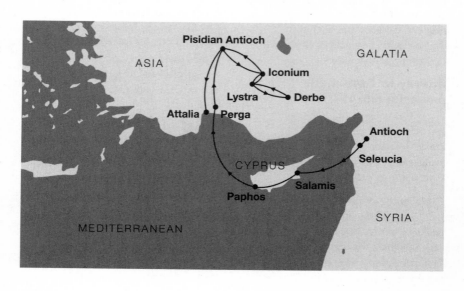

- What do we learn about the church at Antioch?
- What do we learn about God in these verses?

The church at Antioch was made up of Jews and Gentiles (11:20-21). The leadership of the church is also very mixed. Barnabas is from Cyprus (4:36); Simeon is an African ("Niger" means "black"); Lucius is from North Africa; Manean grew up in the king's house, and Saul is a Jew from Tarsus (21:39).

While they were "worshipping", God the Holy Spirit spoke to them. The word for "worshipping" can mean "serving". So this may not mean the Holy Spirit spoke while they were singing. We are not told how the Holy Spirit spoke—only that he did.

God tells the church to set Barnabas and Saul apart for special work. We know Saul had a special job to do in spreading the good news (9:15). God is a missionary God! He wants everyone to hear about Jesus. That is why Barnabas and Saul must leave Antioch.

READ verses 4-12

Verse 6: "Sorcerer" – someone who does magic.

Verse 7: "Proconsul" – a Roman official, governor.

Verse 10: "Perverting" – twisting.

- What is significant about the different people's names?
- What is so sad and wrong about what Elymas does?
- Why does Luke tell us about Saul's change of name (to Paul) at this point (v9)?

The Roman proconsul is interested to find out about Jesus. God sent Barnabas and Saul to Cyprus for people like him. But the Jewish sorcerer opposes them. He tries to stop Sergius Paulus from believing the message of the gospel.

This is sad because Elymas (Bar-Jesus) is a Jew. He should know sorcery is wrong, and he should be pleased to hear the message about Jesus.

Notice the strong words Paul says about the sorcerer. He says he is full of deceit and lies and goes against what is right (v10). He is a "child of the devil" (v10). This makes Elymas' name especially sad. He is called "Bar-Jesus", which means son of Jesus (v6). Instead of being a son of Jesus, he is a child of the devil. All sorcerers are on the side of the devil and are against God's work.

22

So the good news about Jesus goes to a Gentile—but a Jew tries to stop the Gentile believing. We will see this pattern repeated through the missionary journey. The Jews oppose the message and try to stop the Gentiles hearing it.

This is why Luke tells us about Saul's other name. He has only been called "Saul" (his Jewish name) so far. But he will only be called "Paul" (his Gentile name) from this point on. Luke tells us his Gentile name here to show Paul is the apostle to the Gentiles. That means he will face opposition from his own people, the Jews.

God blinds Elymas and the governor comes to faith in Jesus (v11-12). The magician can do nothing to stop becoming blind. The blindness is a picture of how Elymas cannot see the truth. See how no one will stop the powerful message about Jesus spreading.

This is the start of deliberate journeys to tell people about Jesus. God starts this. God wants everyone to hear about Jesus. But in this first story Luke shows there will be opposition to the spread of God's message.

So the main point of the passage is: God wants the good news to spread but there will be opposition.

Find the main point of the passage

- What does this passage tell us about God and the spread of the good news?
- What does this passage tell us about opposition to the good news of Jesus?
- What is the main lesson from these verses?

 **PLAN**

Main point of the sermon

Your sermon will explain the passage, and also apply the passage to your hearers. Look at the main point of the passage. Write what this main point will mean for your hearers.

It will be something like this: God wants everyone to hear the message about Jesus. As God's message is spread, there will be opposition. So we must spread God's message and expect opposition.

Sub-points

- Read the main point again.
- Read the verses again.
- What sub-points will help you teach this passage?

This passage is about spreading the good news about Jesus, and the opposition that comes. Opposition here comes from a Jew who is a sorcerer. But the devil is behind this opposition.

Think of a heading for each sub-point.

For example:

1. God wants the good news to spread (v1-3)

2. The good news will be opposed (v4-8)

3. The good news will not be stopped (v 9-12)

Illustrate

Elymas looks like someone with power and religious knowledge but he is not. He is a child of the devil and tricks people. This is a terrible thing because it deceives people about the most important message of all. Are there people like this in your area that you need to warn about?

Apply

God wants the good news about Jesus to spread. As we spread it, we must expect opposition. The devil will always find ways to try to stop the message spreading.

Sometimes opposition will come from people who should know better. Some people call themselves Christians, but they do not follow God's word. Some mix up Christianity with magic and sorcery. Some twist God's word to mean something different. We need to watch out and know they lead people the wrong way. But we can be confident because we know God will keep the good news spreading.

Review

Check the main point is clear and that you keep to THIS passage.

➔ TEACH

Start

What will happen when the good news of Jesus arrives in a new village or area? Do we expect a good response or a bad response? This passage gives us an example of what to expect.

Explain

1. God wants the good news to spread (v1-3)

God tells the believers in Antioch to set Barnabas and Saul apart for a special job. *Remind people what God said about Saul in Acts 9:15.*

Look at Acts 1:8 and show how Jesus' plan is progressing. Jesus' followers witnessed in Jerusalem, and in Judea and Samaria. But God wants the good news to go to everyone. That is why the Holy Spirit tells the church to send out Barnabas and Saul.

2. The good news will be opposed (v4-8)

Elymas' name means a son of Jesus, but he is a child of the devil. He opposes the good news spreading. It is an example of what we will see again later in Acts. As the good news spreads to Gentiles, many Jews oppose it. We can expect opposition like this today. The devil works through opposition.

Some people called "Christians" may oppose the spread of the good news. They twist the right ways of the Lord (v10) to stop people believing. Paul stands against this and speaks the true message.

3. The good news will not be stopped (v9-12)

Luke gives Saul's Gentile name: Paul (v9). He will be the apostle to the Gentiles. God will make sure the Gentiles hear about Jesus. God shows his judgment on Elymas. God does not judge like this every time someone opposes the good news. But this story shows that God is behind the spread of the good news. Nothing will stop it.

Apply

Challenge and encourage people about the spread of the good news. We can expect opposition, sometimes from people who call themselves Christians. Be willing to stand against them with the truth. Be confident that God's message will spread. *Use your illustration.*

End

God wants the message about Jesus to spread. Opposition will come, but nothing will stop God.

Pray

Pray your church will spread the true and powerful message about Jesus.

↑ STUDY
PROMISES KEPT

Background

We have started a new section of Acts. Paul and Barnabas are taking the message about Jesus to the "ends of the earth" (Acts 1:8). We saw the opposition that comes from Jews as the message spreads to the Gentiles. In this passage we read about Paul and Barnabas visiting Pisidian Antioch (in modern day Turkey). See map on page 108.

Read

READ verses 13:13-52 out loud.

Explain each paragraph in your own words.

Understand

Read verses 13-15

Paul always goes first to the synagogue in a town (see 13:5). Paul and Barnabas are asked if they have something to say. Paul's speech shows us how he explained the gospel to Jewish listeners. He focuses on what God promised in the Old Testament.

READ verses 16-22

Verse 16: "Gentiles who worship God" – Gentiles who worship the true God but have not fully converted to Judaism.

- What important details from the Old Testament does Paul mention?
- What does Paul emphasise about all these events?
- What is so significant about David?

Paul summarises the history of Israel from slavery in Egypt to the time of King David. Paul focuses on what God did. He repeats "God gave", or "God made". This shows the history of Israel is the history of God rescuing and giving (v17-21).

Paul focuses on David (v22). He is called a "man after [God's] own heart" (v22). Every Jew knew God made promises to David. One of David's descendants would be a great king (see Isaiah 9:6-7). That is why the next verse says: "From this man's descendants..." (v23).

READ verses 23-37

- What is Paul's point in verse 23?
- What does Paul tell us about Jesus?
- What repeated ideas are there from the Old Testament?

Paul wants to show Jesus is the promised King and Saviour (v23). John the Baptist pointed everyone to Jesus, who came after him (v25). When people rejected Jesus, they did as the words of the prophets said (v27). They "carried out all that was written about him" (v29). So Jesus' death was part of God's plan. God showed this by raising Jesus from the dead (v30). The people who saw Jesus are now his witnesses (v31).

Notice the repeated ideas. Many times Paul says Jesus fulfilled what God promised. Everything that happened to Jesus was told about before. Paul summarises it in verses 32-33: God's promises in the past have come true.

The quotes from the Old Testament are examples of how Jesus fulfils what was promised to David. Jesus is the king who is enthroned as God's Son (v33, Psalm 2:7). Jesus receives what God promised to David (v34, Isaiah 55:3). Jesus is the holy one who will never see decay, whose body will never become dust (v35, Psalm 16:10).

READ verses 38-39

- What is Paul's conclusion?
- How does this fit with what you know about God's promises in the Old Testament?

Paul's conclusion is that through Jesus, people can be forgiven from sin and set free from the power of sin. Translations of verse 39 vary: Some say "justified"; others say "set free" from sin. The word "justified" usually means "to be declared

right", but here it means "set free" from the power of sin.

Forgiveness and freedom are the key things God promised in the Old Testament (see Jeremiah 31:31-34). Freedom from sin does not mean believers never sin. But we can fight against sin and obey God. One day, after Jesus returns, this promise will be complete and we will be totally free from sin.

READ verses 40-52

Verse 41: "Scoffers" – people who laugh at what God says.

Verse 41: "Perish" – die.

Verse 45: "Abuse" – speak badly of someone.

- What is Paul's warning?
- What response is there to his speech?
- Why does that change the next Sabbath?
- How do Paul and Barnabas respond?

Paul warns people not to reject Jesus. In verse 41 he quotes from Habakkuk 1:5, where God said he would do something so unusual that people may not believe it. The good news about Jesus is so amazing that people may reject it.

At first there is a lot of interest in what Paul says. But the next week

23

the Jews are jealous (v45). They start to talk against Paul and disagree with him.

Paul and Barnabas respond by going to the Gentiles (non-Jews). They quote Isaiah 49:6. Isaiah 49 is about the work of Jesus as God's servant. God says his servant will bring forgiveness to Israel and to the ends of the earth. So God's message about Jesus must go to everyone. The Gentiles happily accept the message, and those who God has chosen believe (v48).

The message about Jesus spreads (v49). But the Jews stir up persecution and Paul and Barnabas must leave the city (v50). As they leave, they shake the dust off their feet. This is a sign that they will never come back (see Luke 10:10-11).

Find the main point of the passage

- What does this passage tell us about God's plans to save people?
- What does it tell us about responding to God's offer to be saved?

Paul's speech focuses on how God kept his promises in Jesus. God now offers salvation through Jesus. But the response to that offer is mixed. The Jews are jealous about the

Gentiles hearing God's message. Many people reject the message and persecute the messengers. But some listen and accept the message and are saved.

So the main point of the passage is that God keeps his promises and offers forgiveness and freedom through Jesus.

 **PLAN**

Main point of the sermon

A sermon explains the passage, and also applies the passage to the hearers. Look at the main point of the passage. Write what this main point will mean for your hearers.

For example:

God is faithful to his promises. God offers forgiveness and freedom through Jesus to everyone who will believe. How do we respond to this offer?

Sub-points

- Read the main point again.
- Read the verses again.
- What sub-points will help you teach this passage?

Think of a heading for each sub-point.

For example:

1. God keeps his promises in Jesus (v13-37)

2. God offers new life in Jesus (v38-39)

3. Be careful how you respond to Jesus (v40-52)

Illustrate

Talk about a promise you made or you know about. It may be a promise of a present or a special trip. You look forward to the day when those promises will be kept. Explain how, in the Old Testament, God made many promises about salvation to come in the future. This passage is about how he kept those promises in Jesus. His offer of salvation has arrived.

Apply

God's plan of salvation is fulfilled in Jesus. God now offers forgiveness and freedom to everyone who believes in Jesus. This is wonderful. We must rejoice and thank God for his forgiveness and freedom. But some people will not believe. So we must make sure we do believe in Jesus. We must be those who honour the word (v48).

Review

Check the main point is clear and that you keep to THIS passage.

→ TEACH

Start

This passage is about the salvation God offers in Jesus. It is the fulfilment of all God promised. *Start by using your illustration. Or you could talk about how God has a plan in history. History has purpose and direction because of Jesus.*

Explain

1. God keeps his promises in Jesus (v13-37)

Paul is asked to speak in the synagogue. He explains the good news about Jesus to a group of Jews. Paul focuses on what God did for his people in the Old Testament. He ends by focusing on God's promises to David (v34-37).

Paul sees these promises are fulfilled in Jesus. *You may not be able to explain each part of the passage. Show Paul's main points in verses 23, 26, and 32-33.* Jesus' death and resurrection fulfilled everything God said would happen. The Old Testament looks forward to Jesus.

2. God offers new life in Jesus (v38-39)

Explain Paul's words in verses 38-39. God offers forgiveness and freedom from the control of sin. This fulfils the promise of a new covenant. *Show people how wonderful these promises are.* This is offered to everyone who believes in Jesus.

Explain what believing in Jesus involves. We must understand our sin and trust God's offer of forgiveness in Jesus.

3. Be careful how you respond to Jesus (v40-52)

Show how the response of the people changes (v42-45). Explain Paul's words in verses 46-48. The Jewish people reject God's message about Jesus—and so they reject the offer of new life. So Paul and Barnabas speak to the Gentiles. God's plan was always that his offer of salvation would go to everyone. *Show the different reaction of the Gentiles who "accept" the message about Jesus, rather than rejecting it.*

Apply

Challenge your hearers about their response. Have they believed in Jesus and received forgiveness and freedom from sin? Do we rejoice in this wonderful salvation?

End

All God's promises of salvation are fulfilled in Jesus. Make sure you trust in him.

Pray

Pray your church will trust in Jesus, rejoice in the salvation God brings and take his message to others.

STUDY
MANY HARD TIMES

Background

Paul and Barnabas are taking God's message of forgiveness through Jesus to the "ends of the earth" (Acts 1:8). In chapter 13 the Jews rejected the message, but many Gentiles believed. The Jews stirred up trouble for Paul and Barnabas, and they were sent out of the region. This passage continues their journey.

Read

READ verses 14:1-28 out loud.

Explain the story in your own words.

Understand

READ verses 1-7

- How do people respond to the message in Iconium?
- What does Luke say about this response (v4)?

A large number of both Jews and Greeks come to believe in Jesus (v1). But some of the Jews go against Paul and Barnabas. The pattern of opposition is repeated. Paul and Barnabas continue to speak boldly about God's grace (v3). God shows their message is true by enabling them to perform miracles.

Luke explains the city is divided. Some people oppose Paul and Barnabas. Some are on Paul and Barnabas' side because they believe in Jesus. The opposition grows and Paul and Barnabas must leave (v6).

READ verses 8-20

Verse 12: "Zeus" and "Hermes" – Greek gods which the people in Lystra worshipped.

- How do the crowd respond to Paul healing a lame man? Why?
- What do Paul and Barnabas tell them?
- How does their time in Lystra end?

The healing of a lame man (v8-10) is written in the same way as the healing in chapter 3. Luke does this to show that Paul is a true apostle, just as Peter was.

People think Paul and Barnabas must be gods. But Paul and Barnabas "tore their clothes" (v14). This shows how upset they are. They are not gods. They are only men bringing the message of the good news of Jesus. That message tells people to turn away from false gods to the true God. God is the Creator and Giver of good things (v15-17). Some Jews from the previous two cities come to Lystra. They stone Paul and think he is dead. But he and Barnabas go to Derbe.

READ verses 21-28

- What do Paul and Barnabas do in Derbe (v21)?
- What do they do when they return to the cities they visited?
- How do they encourage the believers?
- What do they report to the church at Antioch?

The visit to Derbe is similar to other cities. The focus is on their return trip. They strengthen the disciples and "[encourage] them to remain true to the faith" (v22). One part of this encouragement is to teach them about persecution (v22). Suffering and hard times are part of God's plan for his people. This is a sinful world, and those who follow God will face opposition.

Paul and Barnabas choose leaders, called "elders", in each church (v23). The churches need men to teach them and lead them. Paul and Barnabas return to Antioch, from where they were sent (13:1-3). They tell the believers what God was done.

Find the main point of the passage

- What does this passage say about spreading the good news about Jesus?
- What does this passage say about the Christian life?

- What is the main lesson from these verses?
- We see things here that are the same as the last passage. What is different? What point is Luke making here?

Luke focuses on how the message of Jesus causes division. Luke includes teaching to the new believers about going through hard times. The main lesson is about the opposition believers may have to face.

So the main point of the passage is that the message of Jesus results in division, and those who believe in him will face hard times.

PLAN

Main point of the sermon

Write your main point.

The main point will be something like: The good news of Jesus divides and brings opposition.

Sub-points

- Read the main point again.
- Read the verses again.
- What sub-points will help you teach this passage?

Think of a heading for each sub-point. You want to show the different hard times that Paul and Barnabas faced. You also want to encourage believers to keep going.

For example:

1. Believers will face hard times (v1-20)

   - the good news will have people against it

   - the good news will divide

   - the good news brings persecution

2. Believers must keep going (v21-28)

   - stay faithful to God

   - depend on God

Illustrate

Believers have turned away from sin and trusted in God. But we live in a world which rejects and hates God. So believers are like faithful people living in a country that has thrown out its right ruler. They try to live for the true king while others do not. That means there will be division and there will be opposition.

But God will return to rule his world. His kingdom will come. We must keep going and be faithful to him.

Apply

This passage tells us what to expect when we follow Jesus. We should expect division and opposition. Division may happen in families or in villages. Opposition may come from other religions or sometimes from within the church. We must not be surprised, but remember that it is normal. Think of some examples that your people will understand and learn from.

We must keep going. We must be faithful to Jesus. We need to encourage each other to do this. We need to depend on God.

Review

Check the main point is clear and that you keep to THIS passage.

 **TEACH**

Start

Talk about ways opposition comes in your place. There may be division too. How do believers respond?

This passage teaches us that persecution is normal and we must expect it. We will learn how to respond to it.

Explain

1. Believers will face hard times (v1-20)

Explain what happens in Iconium (v1-2). People believe in Jesus but the Jews "stirred up the ... Gentiles and poisoned their minds". *Give examples of times when people oppose Christians and try to turn others against them.*

The good news brings division. Iconium is divided by people's response to Jesus. Jesus spoke about division (see Luke 12:51-53). This builds up to persecution. Some Jews plan to kill Paul and Barnabas. They must leave the city.

Paul and Barnabas teach the good news in Lystra. *Explain Paul's speech in verses 15-18.* Paul tells idol-worshippers to turn to the true God. The Jews should agree with this! But they come from Antioch and Iconium to kill Paul.

This shows the hard times that will face us as we spread the good news and live as God's people.

2. Believers must keep going (v21-28)

Paul and Barnabas return to the cities they visited. Rather than preaching the message about Jesus to new people, they now strengthen the believers. Believers need to be strengthened and encouraged to remain true to the faith (v22). Hard times are part of the journey for believers and we must stay faithful.

Paul and Barnabas choose leaders (called "elders"). These will continue to strengthen the followers of Jesus.

Apply

Tell people to expect hard times as believers in Jesus. The good news of Jesus brings opposition and division and sometimes persecution. We must see this is normal.

Then we must challenge people to be faithful to Jesus. *Call people to strengthen and encourage each other.* We must not think the Christian life is easy.

End

Living as a disciple of Jesus will mean facing hard times. We must be faithful and depend on God.

Pray

Pray you will be disciples who stay faithful and depend on God.

↑ STUDY
SAVED BY GRACE ALONE

Background

Paul and Barnabas took the good news about Jesus to new areas. We have seen many Gentiles believing in Jesus. This raises a question: Should they obey the law of Moses?

The Old Testament law was very important to Jews. Did Gentiles need to obey Moses' law as well? This question takes us to the heart of the good news about how we become right with God.

Read

READ verses 15:1 – 16:5 two or three times.

Explain each paragraph of the passage in your own words.

Understand

READ 15:1-4

Verse 1: "Circumcised" – removal of the foreskin. Jews did this as a sign they belonged to God's people.

Verse 2: "Dispute and debate" – argument and discussion.

- What question is asked among the believers in Antioch?
- What is done about this?

The people who come from Judea are probably Jewish Christians. They say circumcision is necessary to be "saved" (v1). Paul and Barnabas argue with them about this (v2). So they go to Jerusalem to speak to the apostles and church leaders.

READ verses 5-18

Verse 9: "Discriminate between" – treat differently.

Verse 11: "Grace" – God's kindness freely given to those who do not deserve it.

- What issue is argued about?
- What argument does Peter make?
- What evidence do Paul and Barnabas give?
- What extra argument does James give?

The issue is: Do Gentiles have to obey the law of Moses? This included circumcision and other laws about things like what foods they could eat. The question is asked by believers who are Pharisees (v5). The Pharisees are very concerned about the importance of the law.

Peter tells them the events of Acts 10. This showed God "accepted" the Gentiles without them being circumcised (v8). Peter says salvation is by "grace" (v11). God has done everything by his free gift of Jesus. There is nothing more for us to do or to add.

Barnabas and Paul tell everyone what God did to the Gentiles through them (v12). James says this was predicted in the Old Testament. God said he would restore his people (David's tent) and he would include Gentiles in that (v16-18; see Amos 9:11-12).

READ verses 19-35

Verse 20, 29: "Abstain" – keep away from.

- What answer does James give?
- How are the Gentiles advised to live (v20)?
- How does this fit with the reason given in verse 21?
- How do people respond to this message when they get the letter (v31)?

James says Jewish believers must not "make it difficult" for Gentiles turning to God (v19). They should not tell them to obey the Old Testament laws.

James lists four things for Gentile believers to keep away from (v20). Most of them are about which food they can eat. The Gentiles are asked to keep part of the food laws. This is not so the Gentiles can be saved, but so they can have contact with Jewish believers. But they can be different to Jews. For example, they can eat pork, which Jews do not eat. There is more of a challenge to the Jewish believers than to the Gentiles.

The fourth "rule" is about "sexual immorality". This may be wrong sexual activity. The Gentiles must be very careful about this because of their past lifestyle. Or it may refer to rules about who you can't marry, which are mentioned in Leviticus with the food laws (Leviticus 20).

So the church leaders keep clearly to the truth of being saved by God's free gift alone. When the believers in Antioch read the letter, they are "glad for its encouraging message" (v31). They were reassured they did not have to obey the law of Moses.

READ verses 15:36 – 16:5

- What is the result of Paul and Barnabas' disagreement over Mark?
- Why does Paul circumcise Timothy?

These events are part of this same passage. We know that because Luke uses one of his

25

summary phrases in 16:5. So these verses finish the argument about circumcision.

The argument about Mark explains why Paul and Barnabas separate and no longer travel together. We do not know who was right or wrong. But the result was two mission teams rather than one. God can work through our disagreements and problems.

Timothy is unusual because he has a Jewish mother but a Greek father. Jews will think it is wrong that Timothy is not circumcised. So Paul circumcises him so he can take part in preaching the good news.

This shows that while circumcision is not needed, it can be done if it is useful. This is an example of Paul's teaching about becoming "all things to all people" (1 Corinthians 9:19-23).

Find the main point of the passage

- What do we learn about the good news about Jesus?
- What does the passage teach us about what people must do to be saved?
- What does it tell us about defending the truth of the good news?
- What does it tell us about showing love for other believers?

Think about the key point in the passage. It focuses on how we are "saved" (v1). We are saved by God's free gift alone (v11). This must be made very clear.

So the main point of the passage is that people are saved by God's free gift alone.

 **PLAN**

Main point of the sermon

Write your main point.

The truth that people are saved by God's free gift alone must be made very clear.

Sub-points

- Read the main point again.
- Read the verses again.

There is one main point in this passage. You may talk people through what happens and then show the main point.

Or you may divide the passage into sub-points. These can focus on the different parts of the story.

For example:

1. The question about being saved (15:1-6)

2. The answer is God's free gift (15:6-21)

3. Living by grace (15:22 – 16:5)

Illustrate

Think of the difference between something you earn by your work and a free gift. A free gift has nothing expected in return. There is no payback. You do not do anything to deserve a free gift. But something you earn is deserved because of the work you have done. Give an example.

Apply

We often want to add our own work to God's free gift. Sometimes we want to add religious rules and practices. This passage shows clearly that salvation is a free gift. It challenges us not to add any extra requirements to believing the good news of Jesus. It also encourages us to defend this truth if it is under attack.

How you apply this passage will depend on your situation. You may be somewhere where the Roman Catholic church is strong. People may think they need to add their own obedience or rituals to what Jesus has done. Or one group may want all believers to do things their way, and say they are not believers if they do not.

Review

Check the main point is clear and that you keep to THIS passage.

# TEACH

Start

Explain that the good news of how to be saved through Jesus is sometimes under threat. It can be threatened by persecution. But more dangerous is the threat which comes from false teaching. False teaching changes the good news. It twists God's clear message of salvation. This passage is about the good news being under threat.

Explain

1. The question about being saved (15:1-6)

Talk through the story. People come from Judea (where Jerusalem is) to Antioch. They say you must be circumcised to be saved (v1). They think circumcision is important because it is part of the law of Moses. Paul and Barnabas argue against this. They decide to go to Jerusalem to discuss this.

Explain what the "question" is in verse 6. Are there rules we must keep to be saved? *Explain how the good news is being challenged. Point out ways it is challenged in your situation.* People may think they have to do religious ceremonies. Or some may teach there is something extra people have to believe or do.

Use your examples from "Apply" in the Plan section.

2. The answer is God's free gift (15:6-21)

There are three ways in which this challenge is answered. *Show how Peter responds (v7-11).* Peter reminds people how God showed he accepted the Gentiles by giving them the Holy Spirit (v8). *Explain verse 11 carefully.* Everyone can only be saved through the grace of Jesus. It is God's free gift. Jesus took the punishment for all the sin of believers on the cross. There is nothing more to pay or do. This is true for Jews and for Gentiles.

Second, Paul and Barnabas report on what God did through them. They speak about the signs and wonders to the Gentiles. This shows God is at work among the Gentiles.

Then James speaks. *Show how he understands that the Gentiles are included as part of God's plan.* Amos 9 predicts a time when God will restore Israel and will include Gentiles. James concludes that the Jews must not make it difficult for Gentiles who believe in Jesus.

James suggests they write to the Gentile believers. They will ask them to avoid sexual immorality and avoid some foods. *Explain the food restrictions are because there are Jews in every city (v21).* Gentiles who keep these restrictions can have contact with Jewish believers. This does not add anything extra to faith in Jesus.

3. Living by grace (15:22 – 16:5)

Explain about the letter and the people who take it. Show how the letter encourages the believers (v31). You can explain more about the content of the letter here if that is helpful for your people.

Explain that being saved by God's free gift alone means we are free to do things for other people. That is one of the ways God's grace changes how we live. Paul circumcises Timothy for the good of others (16:3). Jews will expect him to be circumcised. So Paul makes Timothy's situation more acceptable. It will make Timothy travelling with him easier. Being saved by grace alone means we can be flexible and do what is best for others.

Apply

Remind people of the truth that we are saved by God's free gift of grace alone. Tell people that salvation is a gift (15:11). All we must do is have faith in Jesus. We must remember that and celebrate that.

Challenge people never to add anything to the good news. Tell people not to think that religious rules or practices are needed to be saved.

Encourage people to make this wonderful truth clear. We must teach it to each other. We must defend it when it is under threat. We must correct any false teaching that twists or adds to the wonderful free grace of God.

Encourage people to live in freedom. That means they are also free to limit themselves and do what is best for others.

End

It is God's grace alone that saves. Be strengthened by that. Make it clear to others. Live for others because of God's free gift to you.

Pray

Pray your church will defend the truth of the wonderful news that we are saved only by what Jesus has done. Pray your church will teach that we are saved by free grace alone.

⬆ STUDY
GOD'S WORK AND OUR WORK

Background

Paul and Barnabas decided to visit the towns where they had already preached the good news (15:36). They argued and went different ways. Paul went with Silas (15:40). Paul also asked Timothy to go with him (16:3). So Paul and his friends are now on his second journey.

Read

🎧 READ verses 16:6-15 out loud and explain what happens.

Understand

🎧 READ verses 6-10

- Look at the map and see where Paul and his team are trying to go.
- Which direction are they forced to travel in?
- How do they respond to Paul's vision?
- What do we learn about God?

God directs them as they travel. They are kept from going south-west to Asia (v6). So they go through the centre (Phrygia and Galatia). They cannot go north-east into Bithynia (v7). We do not know how God directed them. We are only told it was the Holy Spirit who stopped them.

God is sending them west so they go to the port of Troas opposite

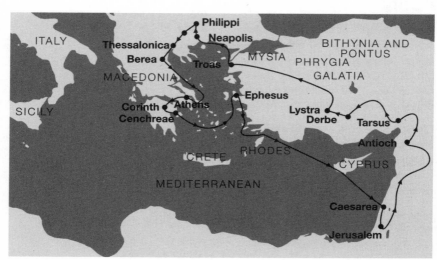

Macedonia (now Greece). Paul has a vision. He sees a man from Macedonia, who asks them to come and help. After this vision they understand that God wants them to preach the good news to the Macedonians.

This is often spoken of as an example of God guiding. It is an example of that. But this is not how we usually make decisions. Paul made many decisions before this vision. For example, he decided to go on this journey and who to take with him. So he did not wait for a vision before he did anything. God guided him as he was going.

We learn that God will direct us as he wants to. We also learn that God is a missionary God. He wants new people to hear about Jesus.

Notice that Luke joins the group at this point. From verse 10 on, Luke speaks about "we".

READ verses 11-15

- Why do they go to the river on the Sabbath?
- What do we know about Lydia?
- How does Lydia come to believe in Jesus?

Paul usually visits the synagogue in a city. But ten men were needed to have a synagogue. If there were not enough, then people met to pray by a river. That is why Paul and the others go there on the Sabbath (v13).

Lydia is not a Jew, but is a "worshipper of God" (v14). She is like other Gentiles who believe in the God of the Jews. Notice how Luke explains how she comes to trust in Jesus. Luke says: "The Lord opened her heart to respond to Paul's message" (v14). This is how people come to believe. People need to hear the message about Jesus, but God needs to open their heart to believe that message.

The result is shown in verse 15. Lydia opens her home to Paul and his friends. This shows that they accept her as a true believer. Lydia's house becomes the meeting point for the believers in Philippi (v40).

Find the main point of the passage

- What does this passage teach us about God's desire for people to hear about Jesus?
- What does it tell us about how people come to faith?

The passage focuses on God calling Paul and his team to preach the good news in new areas. If they go and speak, then God will open people's hearts to respond.

So the main point of the passage is that God wants his good news about Jesus to spread to new people. God will work to bring people to believe.

 # PLAN

Main point of the sermon

Your sermon will explain the passage, and also apply the passage to your hearer. Look at the main point of the passage. Write what this main point will mean for your hearer.

It will be something like this:
God calls us to speak the good news about Jesus, and he will bring people to believe.

Sub-points

- Read the main point again.
- Read the verses again.
- What sub-points will help you teach this passage?

Verses 6-12 show how God calls Paul and the others to Macedonia.

Verses 13-15 show Paul speaking, and God opening Lydia's heart.

You may have sub-headings like these:

1. God wants the good news to spread (v6-10)

2. We need to speak the message (v11-13)

3. God needs to open people's hearts (v14-15)

Illustrate

This passage shows our part and God's part. We speak the message about Jesus; God opens people's hearts. Illustrate this with examples of people coming to faith in Jesus. Sometimes people hear the message many times, but it is only when God opens their hearts that they come to believe.

Or you can talk about how God must work in people's hearts. We can speak the truth, but people are deaf to the truth unless God opens their ears. We can talk about Jesus, but people are blind unless God opens their spiritual eyes.

Apply

This passage encourages us to spread the good news about Jesus. It shows that God wants the message to go to new people. It encourages us that when we speak the message, God will open people's hearts to respond. It keeps us humble—because we know we cannot bring people to believe the good news ourselves. It keeps us confident—because we know that God can bring anyone to faith.

Review

Check the main point is clear and that you keep to THIS passage.

TEACH

Start

Begin by explaining that, for any job, we must know what our part is. In spreading the good news about Jesus, we need to know what we do and what God does.

Explain

1. God wants the good news to spread (v6-10)

Explain how God guides Paul and the others. God forces them west to the coast. The man in the vision is from Macedonia, further west across the sea. Paul and the others understand that God wants them to preach the good news there.

You may want to talk about guidance. Show that Paul's vision is not common in Acts. This is not normally how decisions are made.

Explain what this passage teaches us about God. God wants the good news to spread to people who have never heard it before.

2. We need to speak the message (v11-13)

Explain why they go to a river on the Sabbath. They want to speak the good news about Jesus (v13). We must do this too. We need to speak God's message to people. This is why God called Paul and the others to this area.

Speak about spreading the good news in your situation. Are there places you can go to speak to people? God wants new people to hear about Jesus, and he uses us to do that.

3. God needs to open people's hearts (v14-15)

As Lydia listened to the message, God worked inside her so she believed. We cannot make people come to faith. God has to work in people to open their hearts. *Use your illustration.*

Lydia asks Paul and the others to stay at her house. This is how the church in Philippi begins.

Apply

God wants his wonderful message to go to new people. *Talk about how you can best do this.* God will guide us as he needs to. As we speak, God will open people's hearts to respond. This gives us confidence. It means we will pray for God to work in people.

End

God wants the good news to spread. We speak the message and God opens people's hearts.

Pray

Pray that your church will be confident and humble in speaking the message about Jesus.

⬆ STUDY
GOD WORKS THROUGH OPPOSITION

27

Background

Paul and his friends are on their second missionary journey. God called them to preach the good news in Macedonia so the message about Jesus can spread to new areas (see Acts 1:8). In Philippi, some people have become believers. This passage tells us what happened there next.

Read

🏃 **READ** 16:6-40 two or three times.

Explain each verse in your own words.

Understand

🏃 **READ** verses 16-24

Verse 21: "Advocating customs" – telling people to live a certain way.

Verse 22: "Magistrates" – law officers.

Verse 23: "Flogged" – whipped on the back.

- What are we told about the slave girl?
- Why is Paul troubled by her?
- What do the owners do?
- How does the rest of the city react?

The slave girl can know the future because of an evil spirit. She follows Paul's group and shouts to people (v17). Paul becomes very troubled by this. Probably he did not want the message about Jesus to be connected with this evil spirit. Paul commands the spirit to come out of her (v18).

The owners realise that they cannot make any more money. They take Paul and Silas to the authorities (v19). They say they are causing trouble by encouraging practices which break the law for Romans (v20-21).

The magistrates order a public beating and imprisonment (v22-23). The jailer is commanded to guard Paul and Silas carefully (v23). He puts them deep in the prison and locks their feet in place (v24).

🏃 **READ** verses 25-34

- How do Paul and Silas respond to all this?
- How does the jailer respond to the earthquake?
- What do Paul and Silas say to the jailer?

Paul and Silas pray and sing to God (v25). This is a wonderful sign that they still trust God.

The earthquake opens the prison doors and all the chains fall off the prisoners (v26). Everyone in the prison is free, but no one is hurt. The jailer plans to kill himself. If any prisoners escape, he will be killed as punishment. But Paul shouts that everyone is still there (v28).

The jailer asks what he must do to be saved (v30). Paul and Silas tell him that he and his household need to believe in Jesus (v31). They explain the good news to him and his household (v32). The jailer and his family are baptised and are filled with joy.

Notice what is strange about the earthquake. God does not send it to free Paul and Silas. God sends it so that the jailer will listen to the good news about Jesus.

READ verses 35-40

Verse 37: "Escort" – lead them out.

Verse 39: "Appease" – make happy.

- Why does Paul insist that the magistrates lead them out?
- What do Paula and Silas do before leaving the city?

Paul and Silas are told they can go (v36). But Paul says the magistrates have done wrong. It was against the Roman law to punish Roman citizens without a trial.

The magistrates come to make Paul and Silas happy. Paul probably made them do this to protect the reputation of the church in Philippi. After encouraging the believers, they leave. Notice that Luke says "they" leave. Luke stays in Philippi.

Find the main point of the passage

- Why did God send the earthquake in Philippi?
- What do we learn about God and his plans?

Paul and Silas freed a slave girl from the powers of evil. They suffered as a result. The law officers beat Paul and Silas, and put them in prison to stop them teaching. But God's power brings the jailer and his family to faith.

God worked through opposition to bring more people to faith. People tried to stop the good news going forward but no one can stop God.

So the main point of the passage is: God works through opposition to bring people to trust in Jesus.

PLAN

Main point of the sermon

Your sermon will explain the passage, and apply the passage to your hearers. Look at the main point of the passage. Write what this main point will mean for your hearers.

It may be something like this: God makes sure his good news spreads through opposition.

Sub-points

- Read the main point again.
- Read the verses again.
- What sub-points will help you teach this passage?

The sub-points may be:

1. Wrongly accused (v16-21)

2. Wrongly punished (v22-24)

3. God is still at work (v25-40)

The main point comes from the story of the whole passage, so these sub-points just break the passage into smaller parts.

Illustrate

Give examples of the opposition the good news can bring today. For example, in one city, sex workers were coming to faith in Jesus. This meant they refused to work as prostitutes any more. The men in charge were angry with the people who told the sex workers the good news of Jesus. They arranged to have one of them killed.

Or show how God works through opposition today. Do you know a story where people opposed the good news but the message still spread? In one village, people tried to close down a church. They attacked believers going to church. But the believers kept on teaching the good news. Years later, many people in that village are believers.

Apply

This passage gives us confidence. We expect opposition to come. People will oppose the spread of the good news about Jesus. But God is in control. He will make sure his message spreads. God will bring people to hear the message and respond. That means we can trust God and praise him, even when life is hard. That means we should keep speaking the good news, even when there is opposition.

Review

Check the main point is clear and that you keep to THIS passage.

 **TEACH**

Start

God wants the message about Jesus to spread to new areas. That is why God called Paul and his team to Macedonia. This passage shows the good news spreading, and how God works through opposition.

Explain

1. Wrongly accused (v16-21)

Explain what happens with the slave girl. The owners are only concerned about their money. So they drag Paul and Silas to the authorities. *Explain the wrong accusation they put against Paul and Silas.*

Apply this to your situation. Believers may be accused of doing something against the law like Paul and Silas. Or accused of an attitude like pride or hating people.

2. Wrongly punished (v22-24)

Explain how Paul and Silas are wrongly punished with no trial. Show how the jailer is told to guard them carefully.

It looks as if the time in Philippi has gone badly wrong. It looks as if the message about Jesus cannot be spread any more. *Ask people how they might feel if they were part of the church in Philippi.*

Apply this to your situation. Is there wrong accusation and wrong punishment? Remind people that Paul and Silas suffered this too.

3. God is still at work (v25-40)

Show Paul and Silas are a great example of trusting God even when it looks like everything has gone wrong (v25). Explain what happens with the earthquake. Show the change in verses 29-34. The jailer was meant to stop Paul and Silas from spreading the message. Now, he wants to hear the message. Now, he cares for Paul and Silas.

Explain verses 35-40. Paul is concerned the reputation of the believers will be damaged. That is why he demands that the law officers to come and lead them.

Apply

We are not promised what God will do in our situation. But this passage shows what God is like. He makes sure his message spreads even when it is opposed. When it looks like things have gone wrong, he can turn everything around. This gives us great confidence in spreading the good news. *Use your illustration.*

End

There may be opposition, but God makes sure his message spreads.

Pray

Pray for people facing wrong punishment. Thank God he spreads his good news when it is opposed.

↑ STUDY
TEACH AND LEARN
FROM THE BIBLE

Background

Paul is on his second missionary journey. God has called him to take the good news of Jesus into new areas. Paul and his companions were in Philippi. Now they travel west along the coast to Thessalonica and Berea (see the map on page 130).

Read

READ verses 17:1-15 two or three times.

Read in a different translation if you can. Put each verse into your own words.

Understand

READ verses 1-4

- What does Paul do?
- What is the centre of his message?
- How do some people respond?

Paul and Silas come to Thessalonica. Paul first speaks to Jews and God-fearing Gentiles in the synagogue (v2).

Notice how Luke explains what Paul did. He "reasoned" with them from the Scriptures (v2). He was "explaining" and "proving" that the Messiah (or Christ) had to suffer and

die and rise to life (v3). Paul tried to convince people of what the Old Testament teaches. This means he tried to persuade them that Jesus is the Messiah (or Christ).

Verse 4 tells us the result. Some of the Jews were persuaded. And a large number of God-fearing Greeks and important women believed.

READ verses 5-9

Verse 8: "Turmoil" – disturbance, upset.

- How do other Jews respond to Paul's message?
- What are the believers accused of?
- What is the result?

Some of the Jews are "jealous" (v5). We have seen this before (13:45). They get some "bad characters" together and start a "riot"—a big fight (v5). They cannot find Paul and Silas, and so bring out other believers including one called Jason (v6).

The believers are accused of being troublemakers (v6). They are accused of rebelling against the Roman ruler (Caesar) by saying there is another king, called Jesus (v7).

Think about this accusation. Is it right? Paul and Silas say there is a king called Jesus who is above Caesar. But the believers did not want to rebel against Caesar. They were not going against Caesar's decrees. So this is another example of wrong accusations.

READ verse 10-15

Verse 11: "Noble" – honest, open.

- What is the response in Berea?
- What is the same and what is different between Berea and Thessalonica?

Paul and Silas escape to Berea. Again they go to the synagogue (v10). Luke says the Bereans are "more noble" than the Thessalonians. Their attitude to the message about Jesus is different. They welcome the message with eagerness. They are hungry for it. They look carefully in the Scriptures to check what Paul says (v11).

This group were willing to be taught. They were willing to change their mind. They only needed to see that God taught these things in his word. Many Jews believed, and also many Greek men and important women.

But opposition comes from the Jews in Thessalonica (v13). They stir up the crowds and make life dangerous for the believers. Paul leaves the city but Silas and Timothy stay. Probably, it was more dangerous for Paul. He was the main speaker and so the main target.

Find the main point of the passage

- We have seen Paul travelling and speaking the good news about Jesus several times. What does Luke emphasise in this passage?
- How does Luke show the difference between the Thessalonians and the Bereans?

Luke shows how Paul teaches the Thessalonians and Bereans from the Bible. Some Jews in Thessalonica respond badly. Luke shows the difference between them and the Bereans, who check what Paul says with the Bible.

The main point of the passage is that people should learn from the Bible and believe what God says.

PLAN

Main point of the sermon

Remember the sermon explains the passage, and applies the passage to the hearers. Look at the main point of the passage. Write what this main point will mean for your hearers.

It will be something like this: We should want teaching from the Bible and be willing to learn from the Bible. Be hungry and ready to learn from the Bible.

Sub-points

- Read the main point again.
- Read the verses again.
- What sub-points will help you teach this passage?

You will need to tell the story of what happens in the two cities. But from each story, what point can you make about teaching and learning from the Bible?

The sub-points may be:

1. Teach from the Bible (v1-9)

2. Learn from the Bible (v10-15)

Illustrate

Can you tell a story about some people who are willing to change their minds, and others who will not? You can use the story of Copernicus, who argued that the earth moves round the sun (in the

16th century). But everyone thought that the sun moves round the earth. This was a big change for people to make. Some people were willing to listen and changed their minds. Some people refused to listen and did not change their thinking. They were wrong!

Apply

This passage is a challenge to those of us who teach. We must show people clearly what the Bible says. We must reason with people so they understand the Bible and are convinced by the truth. That is different from telling people what to believe without showing them from the Bible.

This passage challenges all of us to be willing to learn from the Bible and check what the Bible says. So we must be open to change our mind. We may have to change our beliefs and behaviour when we see what the Bible says.

Review

Check the main point is clear and that you keep to THIS passage.

→ TEACH

Start

Paul and his team are on the second missionary journey. Here we see more of how Paul teaches. We see the difference in people's attitudes. This passage helps us to be good teachers and good learners.

Explain

1. Teach from the Bible (v1-9)

Paul speaks in the synagogue. *Point out the words used about Paul's teaching.* He "reasoned with them from the Scriptures"; he was "explaining" and "proving" (v2-3).

This is how Paul taught Jews who believed the authority of the Bible (that it was God's word). Paul taught Gentiles differently *(see v 16-34).*

This passage gives us a model of teaching. We convince people of what the Bible says. We teach the Bible and persuade people about what God says.

The Jews make false accusations (v5-7). *Explain the results in verses 8-9.*

2. Learn from the Bible (v10-15)

Explain what makes the Bereans more noble than the Thessalonians. They are more open to God's message, and study the Scriptures to check what Paul says.

This shows us what we should be like. We must be ready to be taught.

We must be open to learn. We must check everything against the Bible, and study it to know what God says.

Show the response to Paul's message (v12). Tell the reaction of the Jews in Thessalonica and what happens (v13-14).

Apply

Explain that your church must have teaching from the Bible. People must be shown what the Bible says and be convinced. This is different to teaching which only gives the opinion or ideas of the teacher.

Are we willing to learn? *Challenge non-believers if they are willing to change their mind.* Will you see what God says about Jesus? Will you be open to God or refuse to listen? *Use your illustration.*

Also challenge believers. Are we open to learn more from the Bible? Is our attitude like the Bereans? Are we eager to learn, and always check what is taught against the Bible?

End

We want Bible teaching and Bible learning in our churches.

Pray

Pray your church will have Bible teaching and be eager to learn.

⬆ STUDY
THE TRUE GOD

Background

Paul and his team are on a journey spreading the good news about Jesus. They have travelled to Macedonia. In Thessalonica and Berea, they were opposed by Jews. Paul then travelled to Athens on his own (Acts 17:15). This passage is about his time in Athens.

Read

READ 17:16-34 two or three times.

Put each verse in your own words.

Understand

READ verses 16-21

Verse 16: "Idols" – statues that people worshipped.

Verse 18: "Epicurean and Stoic philosophers" – two groups of teachers (explained below).

Verse 18: "Advocating" – telling people to follow.

Verse 19: "Areopagus" – a meeting of city leaders and teachers.

- How does Paul feel? Why?
- Who does he talk to?
- What happens as a result?

Paul is deeply sad because the city is full of idols (v16). Paul knows there is one true God and it hurts him to see people worshipping false gods. Paul speaks to different groups. The Epicureans thought people should be happy. They believed in far-off gods who had nothing to do with people's lives. The Stoics thought there was a god who was part of the natural world. They thought people should be self-controlled and live in harmony with nature.

Some do not understand what Paul says (v18). So they invite Paul to explain his ideas to them. People in Athens spent lots of time discussing new ideas about life (v21).

READ verses 22-31

- What does Paul say about the people of Athens?
- What truths about God does he tell them (v24-31)?
- How does he challenge them (v30)?

The people of Athens are "very religious" (v22). But the altar dedicated to an "unknown god" shows they are ignorant (v23). They do not know the truth about God. That is what Paul will explain (v23).

Paul says:

1. God made everything and is Lord of everything (v24). God does not live in buildings people make. We live in the world he made.

2. God gives us life and breath and everything else. So God does not need anything from us (v25). We depend on him; he does not depend on us.

3. God governs the whole world and wants everyone to know him. The true God is not a statue people make (v29). God made people to be like him. God wants people to turn from their sin, seek him and come to know him.

Paul uses words from Greek poets and teachers (v28). Paul is happy to show where they have something right. But overall they are "ignorant" (v23, 30). Paul says God overlooked this ignorance—but not any more. God now commands everyone to repent—to turn to God as the true God.

God's command to repent is because judgment is coming (v31). Jesus' resurrection from the dead shows this is true. The resurrection showed that Jesus is Lord.

READ verses 32-34

- How do people respond to Paul's speech?

Some people make fun (v32) when Paul talks of the resurrection. But some people want to listen to Paul more. Some believe (v34).

Notice Paul speaks in a very different way to when he speaks to Jews. He does not argue from the Bible. He explains things the people knew—for example, God being creator. He also quotes their writings when they say something true.

Find the main point of the passage

- What does this passage say about knowing the true God?

The people have many wrong ideas about gods. They may have some things right, but they are "ignorant" of God. The true God is our creator, ruler and provider. God wants a relationship with people. God calls people to turn to him.

The main point of the passage is that we can know the truth about God and should believe it.

143

PLAN

Main point of the sermon

Write your main point.

For example: We can know the truth about God and we should turn to him.

Sub-points

- Read the main point again.
- Read the verses again.
- What sub-points will help you teach this passage?

Paul says that we can know the true God. Paul explains what God is like and what God is doing.

You can divide the passage like that.

In your introduction, explain where Paul is and what he sees (v16-21).

1. Who God is (v21-25)

God is our creator, ruler and provider.

2. What God is doing (v26-31)

God calls us to turn to him.

Finish with how people responded in verses 32-34. Use this to challenge and apply the passage to your people.

Illustrate

The people of Athens think they know something about God. But they show they do not know everything because of their altar to an "unknown god".

Think of people like this today. They may be caught up with their customs and beliefs. They have ideas about God, but they need to be taught the truth about him. Explain what people around you believe about God—like following spirits or ancestors.

Apply

Challenge unbelievers on their view of God. Who do they think God is? What do they think he is like? Will they understand that God is their creator and their provider? They may have other customs and beliefs, but this is the truth. Will they turn to him, the true God?

Encourage believers. We see God's control and rule over all people and things. That encourages us to trust him alone and not to follow old traditions.

Teachers of the Bible can learn from Paul how to reach different groups of people. We start with things they know, and draw them to the truth in a way they can understand.

Review

Check the main point is clear and you keep to THIS passage.

 # TEACH

Start

Remind people of Paul's journey and explain that he has arrived in Athens. Explain that people in Athens think they know about many different gods, but they do not know the true God. Paul is going to introduce the true God to them. He will do the same for us.

Explain the gods people follow in your situation or the way they think about God. We all need to know the truth about God, and Paul is going to tell us what it is.

Explain

Use your sub-points to explain the message. Remember to get people to look at the Bible verses.

Begin by explaining verses 16-21.

Paul is very sad to see the city full of man-made idols and false gods. So Paul explains the truth about God in the synagogue and in the market place (v 17). People do not understand (v18).

So Paul speaks at a meeting of the Areopagus—the leaders in the town (v19).

Show that Paul is going to explain the truth about God. He speaks to people who do not know the Bible. So this speech is very different to the ones he made in a Jewish synagogue.

1. Who God is (v22-25)

Show how Paul begins (v22-23). He sees the people of Athens are very religious but they are ignorant. Other religions may have some right ideas about God. But they do not know the true God. Paul will now explain the truth.

Paul shows God is our creator. *Explain verse 24 carefully.* God made the world and everything in it. God is also the ruler of this world (v24). God does not live in temples people build.

God is our provider. *Explain verse 25.* God does not need anyone to give him anything. God is the one who gives us "life and breath and everything else". God does not depend on us! We depend on him for everything.

Ask your people: Do you think of God as needing people? What do the local religions say? Many religions have stories of God needing a world to live in, or needing people to serve him. That is not the true God. God is independent of us, and rules over us. He is Lord. We are made by him and depend completely on him.

2. What God is doing (v26-31)

Explain from verses 26-28 that God wants a relationship with people. God works the history of the world so that people may find him. God wants people to "seek him" (v27).

29

God made us to be like him so that we may know him. *Show how Paul uses the words of the Athenian's poets in verse 28.* We are made by God in his image.

Explain Paul's conclusion in verse 29. God made us to know him. We must never think that God is something we make ourselves.

This all means that God is calling people to him. *Explain verse 30.* God allowed people to be wrong about him. But now God commands people to repent. To repent means to change our mind and life, and turn to God's way. It means thinking about God differently and living with God as boss of our life.

God calls people to turn to him before it is too late. God has set a day when he will judge the world. God gave proof of this judgment by raising Jesus from the dead.

Apply

Show the different reactions (v32-34). Some people laugh, some want to know more, and some believe. *Ask your people what their reaction is. Challenge them whether they know the true God. Challenge people that they cannot make up what they want God to be like.* We must not follow the spirits or gods of our culture. We must understand who the true God is, what he is like, and turn to him.

End

We were ignorant of the true God. But God wants us to know the truth about him. God commands us to turn to him.

Pray

Pray that people will turn to the true God. Pray that they will leave other gods they believe in. Pray that they will trust in only the living God who made them and gives them breath.

↑ STUDY
GOD'S MESSAGE
WILL SPREAD

Background

Paul and his team are on their mission journey spreading the good news of Jesus. They were often opposed by the Jews and sometimes by Gentiles. Yet many people have believed in Jesus.

Paul was in Athens by himself. In this passage, he moves to Corinth. This is where Timothy and Silas join him again.

Read

READ Acts 18:1-17 several times.

Explain the whole story in your own words.

Understand

READ verses 1-8

Verse 4: "Persuade" – change people's thinking.

Verse 5: "Devoted himself exclusively" – did nothing else, gave himself full time.

- Explain what Paul does in Corinth (v1-4).
- What change happens when Timothy and Silas arrive (v5)?
- What do the Jews do and how does Paul respond (v6-8)?

Paul meets Aquila and Priscilla, who have left Rome. They are "tentmakers", making things with leather and cloth. Paul works with them to earn money. Paul tries to persuade Jews in the synagogue about Jesus.

When Timothy and Silas arrive, Paul stops working and uses all his time to teach about Jesus. Timothy and Silas may have worked. Or they may have brought money with them from other churches.

The Jews in the synagogue oppose Paul (v6). Paul cannot continue speaking there. Paul shakes out his clothes. This is a sign of having nothing more to do with them. He has fulfilled his responsibility (v6). The Jews are responsible before God for their response.

Paul then focuses on the Gentiles in Corinth. Many people believe and are baptised. So far, this is similar to Paul's experience in other cities.

READ verses 9-17

Verse 12: "Proconsul" – a local official in charge of law and order.

Verse 14: "Misdemeanour" - did something wrong.

Verse 16: "Drove them off" - threw them out.

- Why does God appear to Paul in a vision?
- What may Paul have been afraid of? What happened in other cities?
- How does God protect him in verses 12-17?

Paul and his team were chased out of other towns. They left because it was so dangerous. But in Corinth Jesus appears to Paul to tell him to stay. Jesus tells Paul to "keep on speaking, do not be silent". He says the same thing twice to emphasise it. Verse 10 gives the reasons why Paul must keep speaking. Jesus is with Paul, and so no one will harm him.

Jesus says this because there are many people in Corinth who will come to faith in Jesus. Paul must stay and speak so they can hear the good news. So Corinth will be different to the other cities.

The promise to protect Paul is worked out in verses 12-17. The Jews put Paul on trial. They say he encourages people to worship God in ways that are against the Roman law. This is the same accusation that was made in other towns (see 17:7). But the Roman official decides there is no crime. That ends the trial and Paul is free to go. This time the synagogue ruler, rather than Paul, is beaten.

Find the main point of the passage

- What does this passage say about opposition to the good news about Jesus?
- What does this passage tell us about God's protection?

This passage repeats themes we have seen before. The Jews go against Paul and the good news of Jesus. As a result, Paul moves to speak to the Gentiles. The Jews make an attack on Paul. But God tells Paul he will protect him. God protects Paul through the Roman law court. God does this because he has many people in Corinth who will believe.

So the main point of the passage is: God protects Paul so that the good news about Jesus can keep on spreading.

 **PLAN**

Main point of the sermon

Your sermon will explain the passage, and apply the passage to your hearers. Look at the main point of the passage. Write what this main point will mean for your hearers.

For example: God will make sure the good news of Jesus spreads to those he wants to hear.

Sub-points

- Read the main point again.
- Read the verses again.
- What sub-points will help you teach this passage?

The passage focuses on opposition and God's protection. God protects Paul so that the message keeps on spreading. So the sub points can be:

1. Be ready for opposition (v1-8)

2. Trust God to spread the good news of Jesus (v9-17)

Illustrate

God wants the good news of Jesus to go to the people in Corinth he knows will believe. So God encourages Paul to keep speaking and protects him from harm.

In American football, some players block the players of the opposing team. They do this so the person carrying the ball can keep running towards the goal line. In Corinth, God used the Roman ruler to block the opposition of the Jews so that Paul can keep speaking the good news of Jesus.

Apply

God's promise to Paul in Corinth is special to him at that time. So we need to be very careful in how we apply it. We cannot say God will protect us from harm and difficulties. Remember that in other cities Paul was in great danger. We can say that, if God chooses to, he will protect us to speak his message. We see that God will make sure the good news of Jesus spreads. We can be very sure nothing can stop God. We must be confident that God is in control. So we must keep speaking the good news about Jesus.

Review

Check the main point is clear and that you keep to THIS passage.

 # TEACH

Start

Remind your people of Paul's journey. In several cities, the Jews were against him *(see 13:45, 50; 17:6-7)*. This opposition meant he and his friends were in danger and had to leave.

Explain

1. Be ready for opposition (v1-8)

Paul comes to Corinth. He works and he teaches about Jesus (v3-4). When Silas and Timothy join him, Paul preaches full time (v5).

The Jews then oppose Paul (v6). *Explain Paul's reply (v6).* He has done his part. They are now responsible. *Apply this to non-believers. If they have been told the good news about Jesus, they are responsible for how they respond.*

Paul turns to the Gentiles. Many come to faith in Jesus (v7-8).

We expect opposition. We must speak the message. But we are not responsible for how people respond.

2. Trust God to spread the good news of Jesus (v9-17)

So far, Paul's time in Corinth is like in other cities. We now expect more trouble. Paul may have to leave. Jesus' words change this (v9-10).

Jesus tells Paul not to be afraid but to keep speaking. It is often fear that means we are silent. Jesus promises protection. *Show the reason for this (v10).* Jesus promises protection so that his people can hear the message. Paul stays in Corinth much longer than other cities (v11).

Jesus' promise is tested. The Jews accuse Paul of breaking the law (v13). We might expect Paul to be beaten or put in prison. But Jesus protects Paul through the Roman official. The attack of the Jews comes to nothing. *Use your illustration.*

Apply

Jesus gives a specific promise to protect Paul in Corinth. We do not know what protection Jesus will give to us. But if Jesus has people he wants to hear the good news, then nothing can stop it.

We are encouraged to spread the message. We expect opposition. We also expect Jesus to make sure his message keeps spreading.

End

Jesus will make sure the good news spreads despite opposition.

Pray

Pray that your church will spread the good news about Jesus. Pray that you will not be afraid but trust him.

↑ STUDY
3 TRUE AND FULL TEACHING

Background

Paul is on his second journey spreading the good news of Jesus. In this passage, Paul leaves Corinth and travels home to Antioch, but he visits Ephesus on the way.

This is the last part of Paul's second mission journey, and the start of his third mission journey. Luke puts these together to focus on what happens in the city of Ephesus.

Read

READ Acts 18:18 – 19:7 out loud.

Explain each paragraph in your own words.

Understand

READ verses 18:18-28

Verse 20: "Declined" – said no.

Verse 25: "Fervour" – energy, enthusiasm.

- Look at the map and follow Paul's travel.
- How do the Jews in Ephesus respond to Paul?
- Why do you think Luke doesn't tell us much about Paul's time in Jerusalem and Antioch (v22-23)?
- What do we learn about Apollos?

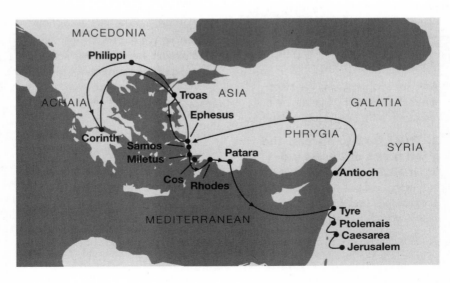

Paul leaves Corinth and sails for Syria (modern-day Turkey). Cutting hair off was a sign of the end of a promise to God. It may be thanksgiving for protection in Corinth, but we are not sure.

The Jews in Ephesus want to hear more about Jesus. Paul decides he must finish his journey but will return to Ephesus if this is God's will (v21).

Luke writes about Paul's return very quickly. Paul visited the church in Jerusalem and then went to Antioch. He set off on his third journey (v23). In a few verses, Paul is back in Ephesus (19:1). Luke focuses on Ephesus.

While Paul is travelling, we read about Apollos coming to Ephesus. Apollos is a well-educated Jew (18:24). He knows about Jesus and speaks true things. But he only knows the baptism of John (v25). He needs to know more. When Priscilla and Aquila hear him, they explain the truth more fully (v26). Notice how humble Apollos is—he is ready to learn more. Notice that Priscilla and Aquila correct him kindly. They are not afraid to correct him, even though he is a teacher who speaks well and is very well educated. Their great concern is for God's truth to be fully and clearly taught.

Apollos is encouraged to go to Achaia. He is a great help in Corinth (the capital city of Achaia). Apollos shows clearly from the Old Testament that Jesus is the Messiah (v28). God uses Apollos' background and learning to make him helpful to Christians.

READ verses 19:1-7

- What is the same about the disciples Paul meets and Apollos?
- What new information did this group need?

Luke tells us about Apollos and this group of disciples at the same time because they are similar. They know something about Jesus but do not know enough. They only heard the teaching from John the Baptist. Paul explains that John's baptism was only to get people ready for Jesus' coming (v4). They had repented, but they had not believed in Jesus. Paul tells them about Jesus, and they are baptised in his name (v5). Now they have the full story.

Today, when people hear about Jesus, they are only baptised once. John's baptism was to prepare people for Jesus and does not happen today. Baptism pictures the new life we have in Jesus when we believe in him.

153

31

When the people believe they receive the Holy Spirit (v6). This is shown by speaking in tongues and prophesying. We have seen this at important points in Acts (see 2:1-12 and 10:44-48). The Holy Spirit coming in this way confirms that people are true Christians. This only happens in Acts when a new group of people believe, eg: the Gentiles. Many people believe in Jesus in Acts and do not speak in tongues.

Some people say this passage teaches that people receive the Holy Spirit as a second step, after believing in Jesus. This is not true as the people here do not believe in Jesus until Paul explains to them.

Find the main point of the passage

- What does this passage say about people needing fuller teaching?
- What does this passage say about the need of teachers?

This passage focuses on people who need fuller teaching. The Jews in Ephesus need someone to teach them about Jesus. Apollos needs to be taught by Priscilla and Aquila. The disciples Paul met need to hear the message about Jesus fully. This need is met by people who can teach the full story.

So the main point of the passage is: people need full teaching, and so need teachers who can give that.

 # PLAN

Main point of the sermon

Write your main point.

Your main point may be: we need true and full teaching about Jesus.

Sub-points

- Read the main point again.
- Read the verses again.
- What sub-points will help you teach this passage?

The passage focuses on people who know something about Jesus but do not have true and full knowledge. The need for teaching is met by people who can teach the full story.

The sub points may be:

1. The need for full and true teaching

2. The need for good teachers

Illustrate

Think of someone who knew something, but not enough. Someone might know a little about engines, but they do not know enough to mend the car. Or they might know part of a journey, but not enough to get to the destination.

This illustrates the passage. The people know something about Jesus. But they do not know enough. They need to be taught more fully.

Apply

Think about those who are not believers. They may know something about Jesus, but still need to know more. Explain how they need to be taught so that they know the truth about Jesus.

Believers who have children, or who teach children, need to be careful. Their children will know some things about Jesus. We must keep teaching them so that they come to a full understanding.

Remember some people have wrong knowledge about Jesus and need to be put right.

Some need to be challenged to respond to what they do know.

All of this means we need good teachers. We need people like Priscilla and Aquila, and Paul, who can teach rightly, and are not afraid to kindly correct others. Good teachers know the full truth themselves and are able to teach others, and correct what is wrong.

Review

Check the main point is clear and that you keep to THIS passage.

→ TEACH

Start

Explain that this passage sees the end of Paul's second mission journey and the start of his third. You may want to use a map. Show how Luke focuses on what happens in Ephesus.

You may use your illustration. This passage teaches that we need true and complete knowledge about the message of Jesus.

Explain

1. The need for full and true teaching

Explain Paul's visit to Ephesus in 18:18-21. Some Jews in Ephesus want to know more about Jesus. God will make sure they are taught.

Explain about Apollos (v24-25). He knows many things about Jesus. But he needs to be taught more. Priscilla and Aquila do this (v26). They give Apollos greater understanding of Jesus.

The group of disciples who meet Paul (19:1-2) only know about the baptism of John (v3). They do not know about Jesus' death and resurrection. Paul fills in their knowledge (v4). They believe in Jesus, and are then baptised and receive the Holy Spirit.

2. The need for good teachers

There is a need for teachers. God uses Priscilla and Aquila to teach Apollos. They give him true and complete information.

Apollos becomes a teacher who is very useful to the church in Corinth (18:27-28). For this to happen, Apollos needed to be taught.

The disciples are taught by Paul (19:4). A teacher was needed to help them know the full story.

We need good teachers who can fully explain God's word and help us have a true and complete understanding of Jesus.

Apply

Non-believers may know something about Jesus. They need to be taught to have true and full knowledge. They may have wrong ideas about Jesus and need to be corrected.

Believers who have children need to teach them carefully so that they gain true and full knowledge about Jesus.

Apply this to your church as a whole. Do they want to be taught? Are they willing to be put right? Do they want good clear teachers?

End

We need true and complete knowledge about Jesus. We need to be taught, and we need faithful teachers who can do that.

Pray

Pray that your church will grow in knowledge of Jesus. Pray you will have teachers who teach the whole truth.

⬆ STUDY
3 2 HONOUR JESUS

Background

Paul makes journeys spreading the good news of Jesus. He has finished his second journey and started his third. Here we read about Paul's ministry in Ephesus. This passage is the end of Luke's fifth section of his book. Verse 20 is one of Luke's summary verses. Luke uses summary verses to divide the book into big sections.

Read

READ verses 19:8-20 two or three times.

Tell the story in your own words.

Understand

READ 19:8-12

Verse 9: "Obstinate" – stubborn.

Verse 9: "Publicly maligned" – openly said evil things.

Verse 9: "The Way" – the message about Jesus.

- What did Paul do in Ephesus (v8-10)?
- What was unusual about Paul's ministry in Ephesus (v11-12)?

Paul speaks in the synagogue as usual. Then, some of the Jews resist the good news (v9). Paul moves to a lecture hall to continue speaking about Jesus. After two years, everyone in the province of Asia has heard the message about Jesus (v10).

God does amazing miracles through Paul. Luke says how unusual these miracles are (v11). People are healed even by pieces of material that Paul has touched. God is confirming that Paul is an apostle—someone given authority to speak the truth about Jesus. We also saw Peter doing extraordinary miracles (5:12-16).

READ 19:13-20

Verse 13: "Invoke" – use the power of.

Verse 17: "Honour" – respect highly.

Verse 19: "Drachmas" – silver coins, each worth a day's wages.

- Explain what happens in your own words.
- What is the result of this event with evil spirits (v17-20)?

Ephesus was well known for people doing magic and sorcery. Some Jews know that Paul drove out evil spirits in Jesus' name. So they try to use Jesus' name themselves. Notice it is Jesus' name that is used because he is where all power comes from. But these Jews do not believe in Jesus themselves. They try to use Jesus for their own purpose.

The evil spirit recognises the authority of Jesus and the role of Paul (v15). But these Jews have no authority. They are shamed by being beaten and stripped of their clothes (v16). People are filled with fear and the name of Jesus is respected highly (v17).

Another result is that some who believed in Jesus confess their sins (v18). These believers now hold Jesus in great honour. They now think of Jesus as bigger and more important. This then changes how they live. They confess their evil ways (v19). They have books which contain spells or magic words. These are very valuable (v19). But the believers see clearly they need to turn away from these evil things.

Luke finishes this section with a summary verse (v20). This marks the end of the fifth section of the book. The summary verse says that the message about Jesus spread widely (remember 1:8). The good news is spreading to more people. But it is also growing in influence; it "grew in power". It is like ripples in a lake getting bigger and spreading further.

Find the main point of the passage

The events in Ephesus are like other cities. Paul speaks in the synagogue, and then the Jews oppose him. As in Corinth, Paul is allowed to stay and keep speaking.

The focus is on the miracles and events with evil spirits. The result is that Jesus is highly respected. This has an effect on the believers. Honouring Jesus means they confess their sins, leave their magic ways, and live for Jesus. This is how the word of the Lord spreads and grows in power.

So the main point of the passage is that change comes as people believe in Jesus and respect him highly.

PLAN

Main point of the sermon

Remember the sermon explains the passage, and applies it to your hearers. Look at the main point of the passage. Write what this main point will mean for your hearers.

For example: The powerful word of the Lord brings change as the name of Jesus is highly respected.

Sub-points

- Read the main point again.
- Read the verses again.
- What sub-points will help you teach this passage?

The sub points may be:

1. The message about Jesus spreads (v8-10)

2. Jesus is honoured (v11-17)

3. People change (v18-20)

Illustrate

You may talk about our attitude to important people. We know that a king or prime minister is important, and so we show honour and respect to him. We behave differently towards a king than to someone else. In the same way, if we truly see who Jesus is we, will honour and respect him. It will change the way we live.

Apply

This passage challenges us to honour (highly respect) Jesus. It shows how some people believed in Jesus but needed to respect him more. They had wrong things in their lives which needed to be thrown out. They wanted Jesus as well as their wrong practises. But that was not right. They needed a bigger understanding of Jesus. They needed to see Jesus as ALL important. So they confessed sin and turned away from magic practises.

Challenge your hearers about their view of Jesus. Is he all important to them? Are there sins they need to confess and turn away from? Are there magic and sorcery practices they need to leave? We must not hold on to evil things. We must follow only Jesus, and trust him for everything.

Review

Check the main point is clear and that you keep to THIS passage.

 **TEACH**

Start

Remind people where Paul is. Paul is on his third missionary journey spreading the good news about Jesus. *Remind people that the spread of the good news is the big message of Acts.* This spread is not only so that more and more people hear it. It is also so that people are changed and grow by it.

Explain

Use your sub-points to explain the message. Remember to get people to look at the Bible verses.

1. The message about Jesus spreads (v8-10)

Talk people through verses 8-10. Paul speaks "boldly" and argues "persuasively" about the kingdom of God. But some of the Jews begin to oppose the message. Paul leaves the synagogue. He holds discussions in a lecture hall for two years.

The result is that everyone living in Asia heard "the word of the Lord". People passed through Ephesus and heard the good news of Jesus. They then passed the message on to their own towns.

This is how "the word of the Lord spread widely" (v20). This is what we want to happen in our villages, towns and cities.

2. Jesus is honoured (v11-17)

Remind your hearers that God gave the apostles power to do miracles. This does not mean that God does not perform miracles today. But it does mean we do not expect them in the same way. Even for Paul, these miracles were "extraordinary"—they were not usual. God decided to show his great power to this city.

Explain verses 13-14. There were many sorcerers and much magic in Ephesus. People tried to drive out evil spirits. They used special words or magic practices. Some Jews try to use Jesus' name. They do not believe in Jesus themselves. They try to use Jesus for their own purpose.

Luke gives a specific example (v14-16). The evil spirit knows about Jesus and Paul. He understands the authority they have. But the evil spirit does not know these other men. These men are beaten and shamed. This shows that the name of Jesus cannot be used as a magic word to get power.

The result is in verse 17. People are afraid and the name of Jesus is held in high honour. They recognise that Jesus has authority and great power. *Explain the idea of honouring Jesus. Help people to feel the change in Ephesus.* Before, people had a low view of Jesus. Now, they honour and respect him.

32

3. People change (v18-20)

Show how Luke tells us the results of this change. Verses 18-19 tell about believers. Some come and confess their evil deeds. The change in their view of Jesus results in a change in their lives. *Use your illustration to show this.*

When we honour Jesus, we will live with him as boss of our life. This is shown in confessing and turning from our sin.

Luke gives an example in verse 19. Some people practised sorcery. *Explain Ephesus was well known for magic and sorcery.* Many of the believers were involved in this. Now that they honour Jesus, they turn away from these evil practises. This is shown by burning their magic books publicly. The value of the books is very high. Point out that people could have sold them. But because now they honour Jesus, they burn them instead. They see how wrong these books are.

See what happens as a result in verse 20. As sin was cleaned out, the word of the Lord spread widely and it "grew in power". The message about Jesus grew in influence over the people. People honoured Jesus, and lived with him as leader of their life.

Apply

Challenge your hearers whether they hold Jesus in high honour. Is Jesus "number one" in their life? How does that show in their lives? Are there sins people need to confess? Are there actions people need to take, like burning the magic books?

End

We want to see the message about Jesus spread and grow in power. That means we need to honour Jesus—we need to love and fear him alone.

Pray

Pray for believers to honour Jesus— to highly respect him and live with him as their boss. Pray that people will confess their hidden sins and turn away from them.

⬆ STUDY

JESUS AGAINST OTHER GODS

Background

Paul has started his third missionary journey spreading the good news about Jesus. So far the journey has focused on Ephesus. A summary verse brings the fifth section to a close (19:20). So, although this passage continues in Ephesus, it is the start of the final section of Acts.

This final section looks at Paul's journey to Jerusalem and then Rome (19:21). A main theme of this final section is opposition to the good news of Jesus.

Read

🕐 READ verses 19:21-41 two or three times out loud.

How can you summarise the story to tell someone else?

Understand

🕐 READ verses 21-22

- What does Paul decide he must do? Compare this with 20:22.
- How does this set the theme for the rest of the book?

Paul decides to go to Jerusalem. Paul says later that he is "compelled by the Spirit" (20:22). Paul says

he must then visit Rome. He uses strong language to say this ("I must", 19:21). This is similar to how Jesus says he must go to Jerusalem (Luke 9:51).

🕐 READ verses 23-34

Verse 23: "The Way" – the message about Jesus.

Verse 24: "Artemis" – a Greek goddess (also called Diana).

Verse 27: "Discredited" – get a bad name.

- What is the cause of the big trouble in Ephesus?
- What accusations are made against Paul?
- What danger is Paul in?

Luke immediately tells us about a big trouble caused by the message about Jesus. A silversmith called Demetrius gathers craftsmen together (v24-25). He tells them that Paul has convinced people that their gods are not really gods at all (v26). So, many people will not worship Artemis anymore. Demetrius says their trade, and the reputation of Artemis, will be spoiled (v27).

This makes the craftsmen very angry (v28). Soon there is a big crowd (v28-29). They take two of

Paul's companions to the "theatre" (v29). This is an open-air area which seated thousands of people.

Paul wants to speak to the crowd but the other believers do not let him (v30). It is too dangerous. There is great confusion (v32). Imagine the noise and anger! The Jews try to get someone to speak. They may want to make clear they are different to Paul. But the crowd shouts for two hours (v34). This shows their anger and confusion.

READ verses 35-41

Verse 40: "Rioting" – trouble caused by an angry crowd.

- What does the city clerk (the town leader) say about the riot?
- Who speaks up for Paul?

The city clerk gets the crowd quiet. He says everyone knows about Ephesus and the temple of Artemis (v35). So they must calm down and not do anything without thinking carefully (v36).

Paul and his friends have done no wrong (v37). If anyone has a charge against them, they can use the legal system (v38-39). The "danger" now is that the crowd will be charged with doing wrong. The "danger" before was that the craftsmen would lose their business and the goddess would lose her fame (v27).

Find the main point of the passage

- Why does Luke write about the rioting here? What is the link with Paul's planned journey?
- What does this passage show us about how the message of Jesus can change a city?
- What does this passage tell us about opposition to the message of Jesus?

The focus is the challenge of God's message to false gods. Jesus has changed Ephesus. That change brings opposition. Opposition is a main theme of the final section of Acts. Paul's life is in danger many times. But God still gets him to Jerusalem and Rome.

So the main point of the passage is: Jesus brings change, and that change can bring opposition.

PLAN

Main point of the sermon

Your sermon will explain the passage, and apply it to your hearers. Look at the main point of the passage. Write what this main point means for your hearers.

The passage focuses on opposition to Paul and his message because of the change it brought to Ephesus. This can be the same where we are.

So the main point is: Jesus brings change, and that change can bring opposition.

Sub-points

- Read the main point again.
- Read the verses again.
- What sub-points will help you teach this passage?

The focus is on the change Jesus brings to Ephesus. This change then causes opposition.

The sub points may be:

1. The change Jesus brings (v23-27)

2. The opposition Jesus causes (v28-41)

Illustrate

Give an example of someone who changed sides. Someone might change sides in a war. Or in sport, someone who goes to the other team. When they go from one side to the other side this causes an angry reaction!

Knowing Jesus brings people to change sides. They stop worshipping one god and start worshipping the true God. When that happens there is often opposition. There can be a battle to try to win people back to their old ways.

Apply

This passage shows the effect Jesus had on a city. Many people believed in Jesus. They stop worshipping false gods. These false gods are shown to be not gods and empty. Apply this to your situation. Are there false gods people worship? Explain how they are not true gods. Call people to stop worshipping them and turn to Jesus.

When people leave false gods, you can expect there will be opposition. Others may fight back. They may accuse believers of doing wrong.

Review

Check the main point is clear and that you keep to THIS passage.

 **TEACH**

Start

This passage begins a new section in Acts. It begins Paul's journey to Jerusalem and then Rome. We will see much opposition to the good news. Luke first tells us about the change Jesus brought to Ephesus.

Explain

1. The change Jesus brings (v23-27)

The good news about Jesus causes much opposition in Acts. This is one of the biggest incidents. *From Demetrius' words show the impact the gospel had on people in Ephesus (v26).* Many burned their magic books (19:18-19). The change is so great that Demetrius is worried about his business.

Challenge your people to think whether they have fully turned from false gods. Do they believe man-made gods are no gods at all? Help them see the change Jesus brings. Jesus can change cities and villages so that they become very different.

2. The opposition Jesus causes (v28-41)

When Jesus brings change, there will be opposition. *Show how this happens with Demetrius and others.* They are worried about their trade and their god (v27).

Give examples from our world today. Some people want their religion to be honoured, and do not like others turning to Jesus. Use your illustration.

Explain verses 28-34. Show that Paul's life is in danger. This begins a series of many dangerous moments for Paul. *Show the crowd is confused and angry (v32).* Opposition to Jesus often stirs up bad feeling and brings trouble.

The city leader tells people they are behaving badly. Paul and friends did nothing wrong.

Apply

Has the good news made a big difference in your place as it did in Ephesus? Be encouraged. Or has the good news made little difference so far? Encourage your hearers that the message about Jesus can have a big impact. What will that be like in your situation?

Following Jesus means leaving old ways and old gods, so there will be opposition. We must expect this.

End

Jesus brings great change. But that change often brings opposition.

Pray

Pray that Jesus will make a great difference in your area, and that you will stand firm during opposition.

⬆ STUDY
WORDS TO
ENCOURAGE

Background

Paul is on his third journey spreading the good news about Jesus. Paul decided to go to Jerusalem and on to Rome (19:21). Trouble in Ephesus threatened Paul's planned journey but did not stop it. In this passage, Paul leaves Ephesus and starts his journey. He does not go straight to Jerusalem, but visits and encourages churches on his way.

Read

🕖 **READ** verses 20:1-12 two or three times.

Read in a different translation if you can. Write each verse in your own words.

Understand

🕖 **READ** verses 1-6

- Look at the map to see Paul's journey (page 152).
- What does Paul do both in Ephesus and as he visits other churches?
- What threats face Paul?
- Why does Luke tell us about the people who travelled with him?

Before Paul leaves Ephesus, he calls the believers together to encourage them (v1). Then he visits churches in Macedonia and Greece (Philippi, Thessalonica, Berea, Athens and Corinth). He speaks "many words of encouragement" (v2).

Encouragement is like teaching, but it focuses on strengthening people in what they know already. The aim is not teaching new truths. The aim is to be stronger in what they already know. We see an example of one of these visits in verses 7-12.

When Paul is about to leave, there is a plan against him (v3). The plan may have involved people on board the ship he was going on. So he decides to travel by land.

Paul has a group of other believers with him. They are all from towns and cities he has visited. These men are the fruit of Paul's work. They now help him in his work. Notice Luke writes using the word "we" from verse 6. This means Luke has joined Paul.

🕖 **READ** verses 7-12

- How does Paul spend his time with the believers in Troas?
- What do they do after the miracle?
- How do the people feel at the end?

Paul spends a week in Troas (v6). On the first day of the week (Sunday) they met "to break bread" (v7). They remembered Jesus' death by eating bread and drinking wine as part of a meal together.

This meeting is Paul's last time with these believers. So they talk late into the night. Eutychus falls to the ground outside and is killed (v9). Paul raises him back to life (v10). This miracle was wonderful. It also reminds of the resurrection hope believers have. Although we will die, death is not the end.

The miracle allows their meeting to continue. They eat, and Paul speaks until morning. The result is that the believers were "greatly comforted" (v12). This is the same word for "encouraging" (v1) and "encouragement" (v2). They are strengthened in their faith.

Luke focuses on Paul's words of encouragement to the churches. The word "encouragement" comes at the start (v1-2) and at the end (v12, often translated "comforted"). This encouragement comes through Paul speaking. The miracle with Eutychus is an encouragement. And it also allows Paul to continue speaking words of encouragement.

Encouragement is to do with strengthening. It is not learning new knowledge. It is holding more firmly to what we know. This will help us to keep going as believers. It will help us stand firm in opposition.

So the main point is: we need to be encouraged to stand firm as believers.

Find the main point of the passage

- What important word is repeated in verses 1, 2, 12?
- What does Luke focus on in what Paul does?
- What can we learn from this about life together as God's people?

PLAN

Main point of the sermon

Remember, the sermon explains the passage, and applies it to your hearers. Look at the main point of the passage. Write what this main point will mean for your hearers.

The focus is on encouraging believers. Your main point may be: we all need words to encourage us.

Sub-points

- Read the main point again.
- Read the verses again.
- What sub-points will help you teach this passage?

This passage can be taught without any sub-points. The main point is about encouragement and that runs through the whole passage.

You may divide up the passage like this.

1. Encouragement through words (v1-12)

2. Encouragement through a miracle (v9-12)

Illustrate

Encouragement is to do with strengthening. Think of something that needs to be strengthened. For example, a wall that is made stronger by putting supports against it. The supports are needed to make the wall stronger. It will then stand, even when forces push against it.

We need to be encouraged as believers. We need to be strengthened. This is not learning new information. It is being stronger in what we know. This will help us to keep standing firm as believers. It will help us when there is opposition against us.

Apply

Where do your people need to be strengthened? Where are they weak in their belief? How can you help them to be stronger? How can you help them to strengthen and support each other?

We need to be strong so we will not fall down when false teachers, or sickness or death come. Help your people to stand firm and strong by teaching them faithfully from God's word.

Review

Check the main point is clear and that you keep to THIS passage.

 # TEACH

Start

Remind people where Paul is and what has happened. This section of Acts is about Paul going to Jerusalem and then to Rome (19:21).

Explain that Paul will do a tour of churches around Macedonia and Greece. This is Paul's last visit to these churches. This passage contains details of that visit.

Explain

1. Encouragement through words (v1-12)

Talk people through the whole passage. Point out the repeated idea of "encouragement":

- Speaking to the believers in Ephesus (v1)
- Paul's visits to churches in Macedonia (v2)
- The effect on the believers in Troas (v12)

Explain what encouragement is. It is not learning new truths. It is being strengthened in what we know already, so we have more confidence and certainty. *Use your illustration.*

Encouragement comes through the truth of God's word. It is part of teaching. *Show how Paul spoke in Troas (v7-12).* Paul had so much to say to them that he spoke all night.

We all need encouragement to keep going as believers, especially when there is opposition.

2. Encouragement through a miracle (v9-12)

Explain the events with Eutychus. Paul is talking "on and on" (v9). Eutychus cannot stay awake. He falls out and is killed. Paul raises Eutychus back to life. *Remind people this miracle meant Paul went on speaking encouraging words (v11).* But the miracle itself is encouraging. It is wonderful for the believers to have Eutychus back. And it reminds them of the resurrection hope that they have.

Apply

We all need to be encouraged. When we face opposition, we need to be strong so that we stand firm for Jesus. *See your notes in PLAN and apply to your situation. Do your hearers need to make sure they meet with other believers to be encouraged? Do people need to speak more encouraging words to each other? Do people need to be convinced that growing stronger comes through speaking the good news about God's word?*

End

We must speak encouraging words to make each other strong.

Pray

Pray that you will speak words that encourage one another.

↑ STUDY
LEADERS MUST TEACH AND GUARD

Background

Paul is on his third journey spreading the good news about Jesus. He is now travelling to Jerusalem. Paul stops to meet with the leaders of the church at Ephesus. This is a very important passage to understand how church leaders should live and lead their churches.

Read

READ verses 20:13-38 two or three times.

Put each verse into your own words.

Understand

READ verses 13-17

- Look at the map to see Paul's journey (page 152).
- Why do you think Luke gives us these details?

We do not know why Paul travelled on foot to Assos rather than sailing. Ephesus was close to the coast but Paul decided to sail past. Paul was in a hurry to get to Jerusalem (v16).

From Miletus, Paul sends for the elders of the church in Ephesus. We know from earlier in Acts that Paul appointed elders to lead each church (see 14:23).

READ verses 18-21

First we see what Paul says about his example.

- List what Paul says about his ministry in Ephesus.
- What example has Paul given?
- What has Paul "not hesitated" to do?

Paul tells the elders to remember how he lived with them (v18). He reminds them of what he did. He did not hold back from preaching "anything that would be helpful" (v20). Paul's teaching involved public preaching and private instruction (v20). The main content of the teaching was about "repentance" (turn away from sin to God) and "faith" (trust in Jesus) (v21). Paul reminds the elders of how he lived (v19). It was with great humility and with tears (see also v31). His attitude and his way of living is important as well as the content of his teaching.

READ verses 22-24

The focus is on what Paul says about his future.

- What does Paul say his future involves?
- How does he feel about this?

Paul is forced by the Holy Spirit to go to Jerusalem (v22). He only knows that hard times lie ahead (v23). Paul knows this is part of God's plan. Paul's only concern is to do God's work of telling people the message about God's grace (v24).

READ verses 25-31

Verse 30: "Distort" – twist.

The focus is on what Paul says to the Ephesian elders about their role as leaders.

- What commands does Paul give them?
- What warnings does Paul give them?
- What pictures does Paul use to describe leadership?

Paul tells the elders to "keep watch" (v28). They are like shepherds looking after a flock of sheep. This is a common picture of leadership in the Bible. They are "overseers", who look out to guard and protect others (v28).

The elders must keep watch over themselves because they may go the wrong way. They must keep watch over the church because of the dangers of false teaching. False teachers will hurt the church, like a wolf killing sheep. This false teaching may even come from among the elders themselves (v30).

Paul tells them to "be shepherds" who guard and feed the flock. They continue the work Paul did, and must follow his example. Paul told all of God's will clearly in his teaching (v27). He now hands this responsibility to the leaders.

Paul reminds them that the church belongs to God. God "bought" the church with his own blood (v28). This means the church is God's and is very precious to him. Elders are trusted to look after it for him. This is a very responsible and important role.

READ verses 32-38

This concludes Paul's speech. It focuses on encouragement.

- What encouragement does Paul give?
- Why does he speak about his own example again?

Paul trusts the elders to God and "the word of his grace" (v32). That means he looks to God to take care of them and keep them faithful. God will do this through his "word of grace", which is the good news about Jesus. This message is powerful to build people up and give them an "inheritance"—a home in heaven.

35

Paul reminds the elders of his example in giving to others. Paul did not live in a selfish way (v33). He worked hard to provide for himself and others (v34). Paul is an example of giving rather than receiving (v35). Jesus said that this is a "blessed" way to live. It is better to give than to get.

When Paul leaves, we see that the elders had great love for Paul. With many tears and hugs they say goodbye. This shows the strong relationships Paul had with people.

Find the main point of the passage

- What are the most important things Paul tells the elders to do?
- What does the work of the elders focus on?
- How can you sum up Paul's commands to the elders?

There are many things said about the work of elders, both from Paul's example and his commands. We need to find the key point about the leaders' role. This is the responsibility leaders have. They must watch over the believers. They are responsible for teaching the church. The teaching must be faithful and it must be caring. The leaders must also guard the believers from the harm that comes from false teaching.

The main point is: the leaders are responsible for looking after believers. They do this by faithfully teaching them and caring for them.

 **PLAN**

Main point of the sermon

Your sermon will explain the passage, and apply the passage to your hearers. Look at the main point of the passage. Write what this main point will mean for your hearers.

It will be something like this: Leaders are responsible to watch over believers by faithfully teaching them and guarding them from harm.

Sub-points

- Read the main point again.
- Read the verses again.
- What sub-points will help you teach this passage?

The sub points may be:

1. Leaders who keep teaching (v17-24)

2. Leaders who keep guarding (v25-31)

3. Leaders who keep trusting (v32-38)

Illustrate

There are two illustrations in the passage already. The first is to "keep watch" (v28). That is a lookout watching for danger—ready to warn others. The elders need to watch out for danger to themselves and to the rest of the believers.

The second illustration is of a shepherd (v28). Shepherds are responsible for the flock. They need to feed the sheep and protect them from harm. If the sheep belongs to someone else, the shepherd looks after the sheep for them. So the elders look after God's people for God. The believers belong to God.

Apply

There are many applications for elders and church leaders. They are responsible for the spiritual health of the believers. They must feed them well and they must guard them well. Stop and think how you are doing in leading the people God has trusted to your care.

Everyone needs to know what to expect church leaders to do in the life of the church and how they should live. The people need to encourage them in their work.

Review

Check the main point is clear and that you keep to THIS passage.

→ TEACH

Start

Remind your hearers that Paul is on his way to Jerusalem. In this passage he meets with the leaders of the church in Ephesus.

Speak about the importance of leaders. Good leaders are so important for the health of believers. In this passage, Paul hands over leadership to a group of elders. With strong feeling, he tells them what they must do and how important their work is.

This passage is spoken to leaders. But everyone needs to listen! Everyone in the church needs to know what the leaders are to do. Everyone needs to support the leaders and expect them to do their work.

Explain

1. Leaders who keep on teaching (v17-24)

Show Paul's example in verses 19-21. Paul taught faithfully—in public and private. Paul said everything people needed to hear—the hard things, too. Teaching is one of the most important jobs of a leader.

Teaching must be faithful to all that God says in his word. Leaders can be tempted to miss out the difficult parts or to change what God says. They must not do that—they must teach all the truth faithfully. The

truth focuses on the good news of Jesus. Paul taught people to turn to God in repentance for their sin, and to put their faith in Jesus (v21).

This work of teaching will be difficult. It will cost the leaders (v19). *Explain verses 22-24.* These only apply to Paul. God has told him to go to Jerusalem. But Paul is an example for leaders today. Speaking the truth about Jesus will mean sacrifices and cost. Leaders must never lead for power, position or money. Leading God's people will mean sacrifice. Paul's only concern is to finish the work God has given him.

2. Leaders who keep on guarding (v25-31)

Explain the words "overseer" and "shepherd" from verse 28. The believers are like a flock of sheep, and the leaders are shepherds or overseers. They are responsible for the flock. They are to feed it, care for it and protect it. There will be danger from false teaching. We must not be surprised by false teachers—we should expect them. They will be like wolves. They will harm and kill the sheep. Leaders must watch out and protect the flock. Leaders must also watch themselves because they could become false teachers too.

Show people how important this work is. From verse 28 explain that the church is precious to God. He bought it with his own blood. God has trusted his church to its leaders, for them to care for it. This is why Paul feels so strongly about this work (v31).

3. Leaders who keep on trusting (v32-38)

Leaders can easily feel this work is too great. *Show how Paul gives encouragement in verses 32-35.* He encourages them to be leaders who trust God.

Paul commits the leaders to God and his word (v32). God will look after them. God's word will build them up.

Paul refers to his own example in verses 33-35. This reminds leaders not to be after money. Paul has not gained from his leading. He has only given. But giving is "more blessed" (v35). So Paul says that, in living like this, leaders will not miss out. Leaders make great sacrifices but they do not end up losing. God brings his blessing. That means leaders must trust God for this.

Apply

You can apply each of the points as you go through. This will depend on how your leaders are seen. For example:

- The need for faithful teaching from leaders. Leaders are expected to understand the Bible well. They need time to study and prepare. They must be encouraged to teach faithfully.
- Leaders will make sacrifices. No one should be a leader for what they get out of it. It will cost them.
- The importance of leaders. Leaders must be respected and valued.
- The importance of guarding against false teaching. Leaders must speak out against wrong teaching to protect their people.

End

Leaders who teach and guard well are essential for the church.

Pray

Pray for your leaders. Pray that they will teach and guard well. Pray that they will be faithful, correct false teachers and trust God. Pray for more leaders like Paul for your area or country.

↑ STUDY
BE READY TO
SUFFER FOR JESUS

Background

Paul is on his third journey spreading the good news about Jesus. He was in Ephesus and decided to go to Jerusalem and then on to Rome. He first visited the churches in Macedonia (in Greece), and then met with the leaders from Ephesus. He is now on his way to Jerusalem.

Luke shows how Paul is following in Jesus' steps. Jesus was determined to go to Jerusalem, even though he knew he was going to die there (Luke 9:51; 13:33). Paul said that he must go to Jerusalem, even though he will suffer there (Acts 19:21, 20:22-23).

In this passage, we see more of Paul's journey and his willingness to suffer for Jesus.

Read

READ 21:1-17 two or three times.

Summarise each conversation Paul has in your own words.

Understand

READ verses 1-6

- Look at the map on page 152 to see Paul's journey.
- What do the disciples at Tyre say to Paul?

- What happens when he leaves? What does this tell us?

Paul travels in short boat journeys along the coast until they reach Tyre, where they wait for seven days. The believers there try to persuade Paul to not go to Jerusalem. This was "through the Spirit" (v4). This probably means the Holy Spirit revealed to them the suffering that Paul will face. The Holy Spirit has done this before (20:23), and will do it again (see 21:11). Paul does not change his mind.

Luke shows a lovely picture in verse 5. Everyone says goodbye to Paul and prays for him. Paul is respected and loved. It is clear that what lies ahead for Paul is very serious.

READ verses 7-17

- Follow Paul's journey on the map.
- What does Agabus say will happen to Paul?
- How do the people respond to this message?
- What is Paul's reaction? What does that teach us?

Paul and his companions stay with Philip the evangelist in Caesarea (v8). We heard about Philip in chapter 8. The prophet Agabus predicts what will happen to Paul—

178

the Holy Spirit has shown him (v11). Agabus ties Paul's hands with Paul's belt. This is a picture of Paul being arrested. The Jews in Jerusalem will hand Paul over to the Gentiles. This is very similar to what Jesus said was going to happen to himself (Luke 9:22, 44; 18:32-33).

Paul's' companions, and the believers in Caesarea, "pleaded" with (strongly asked) Paul not to go to Jerusalem (v12). But Paul is sure that this is what he must do. So he asks why they make it harder for him. They are "breaking [his] heart" (v13).

Paul is ready "not only to be bound, but also to die ... for the name of the Lord Jesus" (v13). He only wants to finish the work God gave him. His own life is not important.

The others see that Paul will not change his mind. They say: "The Lord's will be done". They understand they must accept God's plans for Paul (v14). Paul completes the journey and arrives in Jerusalem (v15-17).

Find the main point of the passage

- What are the repeated ideas in this passage?

- What is the focus?

The focus is that Paul will suffer in Jerusalem. People repeatedly tell him not to go to Jerusalem. But Paul is committed. So the main point is: Paul is willing to suffer for Jesus.

PLAN

Main point of the sermon

Write your main point.

It will be something like: Following Jesus means being willing to suffer for him.

In our sermon we may connect to Jesus' words: "Whoever wants to be my disciple must deny themselves and take up their cross daily and follow me" (Luke 9:23). "Denying ourselves" means not doing what we would choose. "Taking up our cross" means being ready to die. Paul is an example of this.

Sub-points

- Read the main point again.
- Read the verses again.

This passage is difficult to divide into sub points. It is better to talk through the whole story pointing out what is repeated.

Illustrate

Think of someone signing up to join the army. They will be a soldier. They are ready to fight for their country. They are prepared to die for their country.

In following Jesus, we sign up to suffer and maybe to die for him. We must be ready to follow him whatever the cost.

Apply

This passage is about being willing to suffer. The key verse is verse 13 where Paul says he is "ready not only to be bound [tied up], but also to die ... for the name of the Lord Jesus". Is that something we can say? Are we ready to suffer and even to die for Jesus?

Other questions from this are:

- If we know it will be painful to do what God wants, do we give up quickly? Do we look for another way?
- In what ways are we not faithful to Jesus so that life will be easier? Or do we avoid living for Jesus?
- How does our willingness to die for Jesus show itself in our life?

Review

Check the main point is clear and that you keep to THIS passage.

 **TEACH**

Start

Start with Jesus' words in Luke 9:23 about following him. Jesus calls believers to "deny ourselves" and "take up our cross" so that we can follow him. So we must be ready to suffer and even to die.

Paul is an example. Paul is on his way to Jerusalem. God told him that he will suffer there.

Explain

Talk people through the passage. Cover the following points:

Paul stops at two places and has important conversations with the believers. In Tyre, the believers urge Paul not to go to Jerusalem (v4). The Holy Spirit warns what will happen. But suffering does not mean Paul should not go.

In Caesarea, a prophet warns what will happen (v11). This is like what Jesus said would happen to him (see Luke 9:22, 44; 18:32-33). The people ask Paul not to go to Jerusalem.

Paul is prepared to be tied up and to die for the Lord Jesus (v13). Here is true commitment. Paul does not turn back, even when people suggest he should.

Now bring lessons from this.

Paul follows the pattern set by Jesus. Jesus was ready to suffer and die to save us. Paul is ready to suffer and die for Jesus. This is not because suffering is good. But this is what following Jesus often involves. Jesus says following him will cost us (Luke 9:23). We are called to follow Jesus, and that means being willing to suffer for him.

Apply

Your people may already suffer for Jesus. Encourage people that they are right in being ready to suffer. They follow the examples of Jesus and Paul. Encourage them to submit to God's will. Encourage them that Jesus is worth suffering for.

In other situations people do not suffer. But we must still deny ourselves and take up our cross. This means every day. We will give up comfort. We will use our time and money to serve others. We choose to live for God and serve him when that is hard and costs us.

End

We follow a Saviour who suffered. We must be prepared to suffer for him.

Pray

Pray that you and your church will be willing to suffer for Jesus. Pray for specific people facing suffering.

↑ STUDY

37 REFUSING TO LISTEN

Background

Paul is in Jerusalem at the end of his third journey. Paul knows he will face suffering there, but he knows that God wants him to go (20:22-24; 21:10-14).

As Paul travelled, some Jews had believed, but many had opposed him. Opposition has often involved the Roman authorities. Opposition from the Jews and the involvement of Roman rulers are very important in Paul's time in Jerusalem.

Read

READ 21:17 – 22:29 out loud.

This is a long passage, but all one story.

Understand

READ 21:17-26

Verse 20: "Zealous for the law" – strong in keeping the rules of the law.

Verse 24: "Purification rites" – Jewish cleansing customs, which often included making a special promise.

- What does Paul report to the church leaders in Jerusalem?

- What do the church leaders report to Paul?
- What do they suggest he does?
- How do they hope this will help?

Paul tells the leaders of the church about his journeys. They tell Paul about all the Jews who have believed in Jesus. But these Jews think Paul is telling Jews to stop obeying Old Testament laws like circumcision (v21).

Remember that some Jews said that Gentiles must obey the law in order to be saved. The decision made in Acts 15 stated that they did not. That is what James refers to in verse 25. Paul is only against the law when it is said to be *needed* to be saved. Paul believes Jewish believers may keep the law—but Jesus is all that is needed to be saved.

The church leaders in Jerusalem suggest Paul takes part in a Jewish ceremony. This will show he respects the Jewish law (v24).

READ verses 27-36

Verse 27: "Seized" – took hold of.

Verse 28: "Defiled" – made unholy.

Verse 30: "Aroused" – stirred up.

Verse 32: "Rioters" – people causing trouble.

- What is Paul accused of?
- How does this fit with verses 17-26?
- How dangerous is the situation?

It is Jews from Asia (places like Ephesus) who stir up the crowd (v27). They may have followed Paul on his journey to Jerusalem.

Paul is accused of teaching against the Jewish people, law and temple (v28). They also say Paul brought a Gentile into the temple (v28-29). This was wrong and could result in death. Paul is dragged out of the temple. They try to kill him (v31).

Paul is saved by the Roman commander (v32). He takes Paul into the barracks (where soldiers live). The anger of the crowd is so great that Paul is kept safe by soldiers carrying him (v35).

READ 21:37 – 22:21

22:3: "Gamaliel" – a respected Jewish teacher.

Verse 4: "Followers of this Way" – people who believe in Jesus.

- Why does Luke tell us about the Roman commander making a mistake about who Paul is?
- Why does Luke repeat the story of Paul coming to know Jesus (which we read in chapter 9)?

- What important details does Paul include to explain himself to the Jews?

To the Romans, Paul looks like a rebel leader, but he is nothing like that. Paul asks to speak to the crowd. He wants to persuade them that he did nothing wrong. He also wants to persuade them about Jesus.

Paul tells the crowd he was as committed to God as they are (v3-5). So he persecuted people who believed in Jesus. Paul did what these Jews are doing to him. Paul explains how Jesus appeared to him. This means Jesus is alive. It means that when Paul persecuted believers, he was persecuting Jesus.

Paul explains how he was taken into Damascus (v10-11). God used Ananias, who was a well-respected Jewish Christian, to speak to him (v12). Ananias explained God's will to Paul (v14-16). Paul had seen the Messiah (or Christ) and was to tell others (v14-15). Notice that God is called the "God of our ancestors [or fathers]" (v14). Paul shows the Jews that it is their God at work.

Paul reports how Jesus sent him away from Jerusalem (v17-21). Paul says the Jews should accept him

37

because his changed life showed it was God at work. But Jesus says he will send Paul to the Gentiles (non-Jews, v21). It is because the Jews will not accept Paul's message that he goes to the Gentiles.

READ 22:22-29

- Why do the Jews shout in protest at this point of the speech?
- How does Paul escape being flogged (beaten up)?
- Why does Luke give these details?

The Jews call for Paul's death (v22). Throwing their coats and dust shows they reject Paul (v23). They reject him because he spoke of going to the Gentiles. They cannot believe God included Gentiles in his plan to save people.

The commander wants to find out what is happening, and so plans to have Paul beaten and questioned (v24). Paul says he is a Roman citizen (v25). This immediately stops the beating because it was against the law to punish Roman citizens without proving them guilty first.

Find the main point of the passage

- What are the repeated ideas? Look at 21:24, 28; 22:17-18.
- What is the connection between what Paul says and how the crowd responds?

The overall picture is that Paul's actions are taken in the wrong way and he is wrongly treated. Paul tried to show his respect for the Jewish law, but he is falsely accused. He gives reasons to show that the message of Jesus is from God. But people will not listen to him. This is what Paul explains in his speech (22:17-21).

The main point is: People refuse to listen to what Paul says.

 **PLAN**

Main point of the sermon

Write down your main point.

Your main point could be: Some people will refuse to listen to the good news of Jesus, but we must keep trying to tell them.

Sub-points

- Read the main point again.
- Read the verses again.
- What sub-points will help you teach this passage?

The sub points may be:

1. Paul shows respect but is wrongly accused (21:17-36)

2. Paul tries to explain but people will not listen (21:37-22:29)

These points explain the passage. You will then need to show how they apply to us today.

Illustrate

Give an example of someone who did something good for good reasons—but people were against him, so they took it the wrong way. They did not listen to any explaining because they wanted to cause trouble for the person. This showed what they think and feel about the person. There was nothing the person could do to persuade them.

Here, the Jews have made up their minds against Paul. They are not willing to listen to his reasons and how it is God at work.

Apply

Remember, this is a very specific situation. This is telling how the opposition between Paul and the Jews grew. But opposition is seen today. Some people will not listen to the good news about Jesus. They may respond in anger and hatred. We try to show respect as Paul does. We try to explain the good news and persuade them. But we must not be surprised when people continue to reject the message.

Review

Check the main point is clear and that you keep to THIS passage.

 **TEACH**

Start

You may start with your illustration. Explain how some people are not willing to listen. They may be worried about different ideas, or not like the person. So they will not listen to what he says. That is what we will see in this passage.

Remind people what happened so far. Paul planned this journey to Jerusalem in chapter 19. On his way there was strong opposition from some Jews. Paul was warned he would be handed over to Roman rulers and be badly treated.

Paul has arrived in Jerusalem, and we see what happens.

Explain

1. Paul shows respect but is wrongly accused (21:17-36)

Explain the concern of the Christian leaders (elders) in verses 17-21. Remind people of the background of Acts 15. Paul is not against the Jewish law. But he is against people saying that keeping the law is necessary to be saved. Paul does not teach Jews they should not obey the law. *Explain what the elders suggest (v22-25).* Paul will publicly show his respect for the law.

Explain what happens in verses 27-29. Jews from Asia accuse Paul of teaching against the Jews, against the law and against the temple.

Show how wrong this is. Paul is showing respect for the Jewish law, but is accused of being against it. Paul is accused of bringing a Greek into the temple. But he has not done this.

Explain verses 30-36. Show how Paul's life is in danger. Paul is only saved by the Roman commander. *Show how Luke shows that the anger of the crowd is growing.* Paul has to be carried because the crowd is trying to kill him.

Sum up what we have seen. Paul showed respect for the Jewish law but he was wrongly accused. People are not willing to listen to the truth.

2. Paul tries to explain but people will not listen (21:37 – 22:29)

Explain 21:37-39. The Roman commander mistakes who Paul is. This shows that people are confused about who Paul is. Paul asks to speak to the crowd, even though they have tried to kill him. Paul wants to persuade them it is God at work.

Explain Paul's speech. Show the way in which he points out that he also once persecuted believers. He understands why they are so angry with him. *Show how Paul tries to persuade them.* He shows how the God of the Jews is at work. Jesus warned Paul that people in Jerusalem would not accept his message. *Show how Paul tried to convince Jesus that people should accept his message, because he was once like them and persecuted believers (22:19-20)!*

Explain the crowds' reaction in 22:22. They hate the thought of Gentiles being part of God's kingdom.

Go through 22:23-29. Again, people misunderstand who Paul is. The Roman commander does not think that Paul is a Roman citizen. So both the crowd and the Roman commander misunderstand Paul.

Apply

Show people that this is a very specific situation. It is how the opposition to Paul from the Jews grew and grew. It teaches us two key lessons. Some people will refuse to listen. They will get hold of wrong ideas. They have already decided what they think. We should be sad about that, but not surprised.

We can do what Paul does. We must show respect for people. We should try to explain to them. *Does this need to happen where you are? Are there groups who are set against you? Do some people misunderstand? What can you do to show respect? How can you explain things to them?*

End

Some people will refuse to listen, but we will show respect and try to explain.

Pray

Pray for people who are against you. Ask God to be very kind to them and open their eyes. Pray for strength to show respect and to explain the good news to them.

↑ STUDY
GOD'S PLANS CAN'T BE STOPPED

Background

Paul is in Jerusalem. He knows he will suffer there (20:22-23; 21:11). Paul tried to show his respect for the Jewish law (21:22-24, 26). But some of the Jews tried to kill him. Paul was saved by a Roman commander. Paul explained to the Jewish crowd how Jesus changed his life. He did this to persuade them it was God at work. They responded with protests and anger.

The Roman commander does not understand what the arguments are about. He wants to find out. So in this passage he arranges for Paul to speak to the Sanhedrin (the Jewish council).

Read

🕭 READ 22:30 – 23:35 out loud.

Summarise the whole story in your own words.

Understand

🕭 READ 22:30 – 23:11

23:1: "Good conscience" – honest heart.

Verse 3: "Violate" – break.

Verse 7: "Dispute" – argument.

- What does the Roman commander want to find out?
- Why is Paul hit across the mouth (v2)?
- Why does Paul apologise (say sorry) (v5)?
- Why does Paul talk about the resurrection?

The Roman commander wants to find out why the crowd are against Paul. All the trials in the next chapters are about the same question of what Paul is accused of. The commander calls the Sanhedrin. This is a council that is in charge of Jewish life.

Paul begins by saying he has "fulfilled his duty to God" (v1). Paul means he has done what is right before God. The high priest orders Paul to be hit. He thinks Paul is guilty. He will not allow Paul to claim to obey God.

Paul calls the high priest a "whitewashed wall". The picture is of something that looks clean on the outside but is unclean inside. The high priest claims that he is judging Paul according to the law. But in ordering Paul to be hit, he breaks the law himself.

Paul then apologises (v5). He did not know it was the high priest speaking and he knows that respect must be shown for the position of high priest. Paul quotes Exodus 22:28 and again shows that he respects the Jewish law.

Paul states the reason for his trial. It is because of his hope in the resurrection (v6). This causes arguments in the Sanhedrin. Luke explains that the Pharisees believed in the resurrection of the dead, but the Sadducees did not. Paul knew this. Luke tells us that this is why Paul raised the issue (v6). But Paul's main belief is that the resurrection of the dead started in Jesus. In the following trials, Paul returns to this claim about the resurrection (see 24:14-15; 26:6-8).

Some Pharisees defend Paul (23:9). They think God may have spoken to him. The argument in the Sanhedrin becomes so angry that the commander again worries for Paul's safety.

That night the Lord Jesus appears to Paul (v11). Jesus encourages Paul. Paul has witnessed already in Jerusalem. He will do so in Rome.

READ verses 12-22

Verse 12: "Conspiracy" – secret plan.

Verse 15, 20: "Pretext" – false reason.

- What is most worrying about this plot against Paul?
- How does God protect Paul?

A large group of Jews plan to kill Paul. They make a strong promise not to eat or drink until he is dead (v12). They ask the high priest and the Sanhedrin to ask ("petition") the commander to bring Paul to them again. They will kill him on the way. This is the greatest threat so far to Paul.

But God protects Paul. The son of Paul's sister hears about the plan (v16). He explains the plot to the commander (v19-21). Notice that the promise the men made is repeated a third time (v12, 14, 21). This shows their commitment to killing Paul.

READ verses 23-35

- How does the Roman commander respond to this threat?
- What does he say in his letter to Governor Felix?
- What is going to happen next?

The commander organises a large number of soldiers. He knows this is a big threat and he wants to prevent

38

anyone from attacking Paul. Paul is taken to Caesarea. This is the start of his journey to Rome. This protection and travel to Rome is what Jesus promised (v11).

The letter from the commander explains the events in Jerusalem. The commander changes some details. He says he knew Paul was a Roman citizen (v27), which was not true. We learn that he passes the case on to the Roman Governor, Felix. Paul's accusers will have to present their charges to Felix (v30). Felix reads the letter and checks where Paul is from. This is to confirm that Felix will judge the case. Paul is left to wait for another trial.

Find the main point of the passage

- What are the repeated ideas in the passage?
- What example does Paul give us?
- What does God do?

We see how bold Paul is before the Jewish council. Luke shows how Paul focuses on the important issue—the resurrection. This results in a threat to his life in the Jewish council and then the plan to kill him. Paul has to trust God. Jesus encourages Paul he will witness in Rome. God works to save Paul. This shows that God is completely in control. The

opposition and threats cannot stop God's plans for Paul.

So the main point is: God's plan for Paul cannot be stopped. Paul will witness about Jesus as God promised.

 PLAN

Main point of the sermon

Write your main point.

It might be: God's plans will always come true, whatever happens. God's plans cannot be stopped.

Sub-points

- Read the main point again.
- Read the verses again.
- What sub-points will help you teach this passage?

We see that Paul is bold to speak the truth about Jesus, even though it brings him into danger (v1, 6). We see the need to trust God's plans, especially in the face of danger and threats.

The sub points can be:

1. Be bold about Jesus (22:30 – 23:10)

2. Trust God to work out his plan (23:11-35)

Illustrate

Use examples in the passage. There is Paul's example of boldness and courage. Do you know of a situation where someone spoke out for what is right, even though there was pressure not to cause trouble?

We also see God protecting Paul in this passage. God has saved people through angels (chapter 12) and earthquakes (chapter 16). But here, God uses the son of Paul's sister. God makes sure the young man is in the right place at the right time to hear the plan. Do you know of "ordinary" things which turned out to be very important? Has someone been in the right place at the right time so that danger was avoided, or someone was helped? These are examples of God at work.

Apply

God's plans cannot be stopped. That means we can be bold about Jesus. We must not be stopped from talking about him. We must be bold and respectful like Paul (1 Peter 3:15).

We can be confident. We know God will achieve his plans. For Paul that meant being rescued to witness for Jesus in Rome. We do not know what God's plans are for us. That means we are not promised protection. But we can still be confident because nothing can stop God's plans.

Review

Check the main point is clear and that you keep to THIS passage.

→ TEACH

Start

Remind people what has happened so far. Paul has been wrongly arrested in Jerusalem. Paul's life is in great danger. He may have felt very afraid. *How do your people feel? Do they need to be encouraged that God's plans cannot be stopped?*

Explain

1. Be bold about Jesus (22:30 – 23:10)

Explain the meeting of the Jewish council to find out what Paul has done wrong. Paul is bold in his opening statement. Paul claims he only kept his duty to God.

Paul responds with boldness when he is hit. *Explain why Paul apologises.* Paul thinks being hit was wrong. But he recognises the authority of the high priest.

Explain the different beliefs of the Pharisees and Sadducees. Jesus' resurrection shows that he is the Messiah (Christ). Paul boldly and clearly says what the main problem is between him and the Jews.

2. Trust God to work out his plan (23:11-35)

Explain Jesus' words to Paul (v11). Paul was afraid and Jesus encourages him. Jesus is pleased with Paul for his bold words. Jesus promises Paul he will get to Rome.

Immediately, there is another threat to Paul's life. *Show how dangerous*

the plan to kill him is. But Jesus keeps his promise to get Paul to Rome. That happens through the son of Paul's sister (v16). This is a wonderful example of God's plans being worked out through ordinary people.

Paul travels to Caesarea under heavy guard. He is one of the safest men in Jerusalem! *Show how the rest of the passage gets ready for the trials which will follow.*

Apply

Apply the two points. We can learn to be bold like Paul. We should show respect but also be willing to point out the truth.

We trust God that his plans cannot be stopped. We do not have a specific promise like Paul. But God is in control, and he will protect and use us as he chooses. We trust God to work out his plans when things look impossible and we do what we can, as Paul did.

End

Be bold to speak clearly for Jesus. In doing this, trust that God's plans cannot be stopped.

Pray

Pray that you and your people will show boldness and trust.

↑ STUDY
DEFEND AND TELL THE TRUTH

Background

In Jerusalem, Paul was rescued twice from Jews who tried to kill him. The Roman commander in Jerusalem sent Paul to the Roman Governor, Felix, in Caesarea. Paul's accusers will present their case to him. Paul will have to defend himself again.

Read

READ 24:1-27 two or three times.

Explain each part of Paul's speech in your own words.

Understand

READ verses 1-9

Verse 3: "Profound gratitude" – deep thanks.

Verse 5: "Sect" – a group which split away from Judaism.

Verse 6: "Desecrate" – spoil.

- Why does Tertullus begin with his words in verses 2-4?
- What is the accusation against Paul?

The Jewish group want to make sure Paul is convicted. Their lawyer, Tertullus, says what a great governor Felix is! He says Felix has brought "peace". His main accusation will be that Paul has spoiled this peace.

Tertullus says Paul is a "troublemaker" responsible for riots and fights (v5). Remember there were riots in many places Paul visited, but Paul was not to blame. Paul is a leader in the "Nazarene sect"—the people who believe in Jesus. They say this group is causing trouble.

The main accusation is that Paul tried to spoil the temple (v6)—see 21:27-29. The other Jews who travelled with Tertullus add to what he said (v9).

READ verses 10-21

- What does Paul say about his recent actions in Jerusalem?
- What does he say is not true?
- What does he admit is true?

Paul defends himself against the charges to do with the temple. He did nothing wrong and no one can prove any of the charges (v12-13).

Paul admits he worships "the God of our ancestors as a follower of the Way" (this means he is a believer in Jesus). He believes the Law and the Prophets (v14). He has the same hope as the Jews in a future resurrection (v15). Paul argues that he is not a dangerous false teacher. But, as a follower of the Way, he believes Jesus is the Messiah (or Christ). Paul tries to keep an honest heart before God and people (v16). He avoids doing anything wrong.

Paul explains why he came to Jerusalem and says he is innocent (v17-18). The people responsible are Jews from Asia (see 21:27). Before the Sanhedrin, Paul only said that he believed in the resurrection (24:21)—see 23:6-10.

READ 24:22-27

Verse 22: "Well acquainted" – knew much about.

- How does Felix respond to all this?
- What does Paul speak about with Felix later?

Felix decides to wait for the Roman commander from Jerusalem (v22). Later, Felix and his wife listen to Paul. Paul speaks about faith in Christ Jesus (v24). That is belief in Jesus as the Christ or Messiah. He also speaks about righteousness, self-control and the judgment to come (v25). Paul challenges Felix and his wife about their need for forgiveness through Jesus.

Felix becomes afraid (v25). He leaves Paul in prison hoping for a bribe. Festus takes over as governor but leaves Paul in prison.

Find the main point of the passage

- What are the main things Paul does?
- How does this fit with the accusations made earlier?

Paul defends his actions and defends the good news about Jesus. Paul argues that he teaches what the Old Testament promised. But he believes the Old Testament's promises are fulfilled (come true) in Jesus. Then Paul takes the opportunity to teach the good news to Felix and Drusilla.

The main point is about how Paul defends the good news of Jesus. Paul also takes the opportunity to teach the good news when he can. The main point is about defending the truth and telling the truth.

PLAN

Main point of the sermon

Write your main point.

Your main point may be something like: we must defend the good news of Jesus against accusations. We must tell out the good news whenever we can.

Sub-points

- Read the main point again.
- Read the verses again.
- What sub-points will help you teach this passage?

The sub points can be:

1. Expect to be accused (v1-9)

2. Be ready to defend the good news (v10-23)

3. Take every opportunity to tell about Jesus (verses 24-27)

Illustrate

In a war, you need to defend yourself against the enemy. What defence you use will depend on the type of attack. You will do whatever is needed to defend against different attacks. For example, soldiers wear armour to protect them from the missiles of the enemy.

So in the trials, Paul defends himself against accusations. Paul responds to whatever accusations are made against him and against the good news about Jesus.

Apply

We can expect the good news of Jesus to be attacked in different ways. We must be ready to defend it. That will often mean defending ourselves and speaking for the truth. Attacks against the good news often involve accusation against the people who speak it. We must not react in a wrong or angry way to accusations against us. Like Paul, we must be ready to quietly explain what we did and how we did it.

This shows how important an honest and pure life is. We should be able to say, as Paul did, that we try to have a clean heart before God and people (v16).

We will always look for opportunities to tell out the good news about Jesus so that people can come to believe in Jesus.

Review

Check the main point is clear and that you keep to THIS passage.

 **TEACH**

Start

Remind people what happened so far. Paul is now on trial in front of the Roman Governor, Felix. The Jews accuse him again, but Paul defends himself and his actions.

Explain

Use your sub-points to explain the message. Get your hearers to look at the Bible verses.

1. Expect to be accused (v1-9)

Show how determined the Jews are. They bring a lawyer to help them in their case against Paul. The lawyer begins by saying nice things about Felix and the peace the Roman governor brought.

Explain the accusations against Paul in verses 5-8. They say Paul is a troublemaker; he is a leader in the "Nazarene sect"; he tried to spoil the temple. Show how difficult and dangerous the situation is for Paul.

Apply this to your situation. Do not be surprised to find people attacking the good news about Jesus. That often means accusing those who spread that message. That will come in different ways. False accusations can be completely untrue, or they may be close to the truth but twisted. That is what happens to Paul. There were riots he was involved in—but he was not

responsible. He was in the temple—but he was not spoiling it. Or accusations may be about attitude—that believers are proud or stupid.

2. Be ready to defend the good news (v10-23)

Show how Paul defends himself. He did nothing wrong at the temple and there is no evidence against him (v13).

Paul happily admits he worships God as a "follower of the Way" (v14). He shows that the true difference between him and the Jews is about belief in God. Paul believes the Old Testament is fulfilled (comes true) in Jesus (v14-15). That is the real issue the Jews are angry about. They do not believe Jesus is the Messiah.

Paul can say he tries to keep an honest heart before God and people (v16). We want to be able to say that. We want to do what is right before God and people around us, so no accusation against us is true.

Paul explains his visit to Jerusalem (v17-18). He says it is the Jews from Asia who did wrong (v19). The real argument is about what he teaches (v20-21).

Felix does not make a judgment. He does not think Paul did wrong, as he does not punish him (v23). Felix is weak and afraid of upsetting the Jews. That is why he leaves Paul in prison.

39

3. Take every opportunity to tell about Jesus (v24-27)

Felix visits Paul with his wife. His wife is Jewish, so she knows Old Testament teaching. Show how Paul tells the good news to Felix and Drusilla (v24-25). Felix feels afraid and stops the conversation. Notice how Paul takes every opportunity to tell the good news about Jesus.

Apply

The main point is that we must be ready to defend the good news. That may mean defending ourselves against accusations. Talk about what people accuse you and your hearers of. Sometimes, those will be very specific and come to court, as with Paul. Other times, they will be less threatening and dangerous. For the honour of God, we must be able to say we did nothing wrong. This shows how very important it is for believers to live honest and pure lives. We must always defend ourselves in a godly way. We must not be angry and rude.

We should be ready for unjust decisions. Paul should have been released, but he was not.

We can be encouraged God will provide opportunities to speak the good news to people. We must be ready to take those opportunities.

End

Be ready to defend the good news against false accusation. Be ready to tell out the good news of Jesus.

Pray

Pray for your people. Pray for courage to defend yourselves. Pray for opportunities to tell out the good news.

↑ STUDY
PERSUADE PEOPLE TO BELIEVE

Background

Think about what happened in the last chapters:

- How many trials has Paul had?
- Who is against him?
- What were the accusations against him?

Paul was accused by Jews of being a troublemaker. The Roman authorities found he did nothing wrong, but he was left in prison. Festus became the new governor (24:27). So the Jews now bring their accusations again.

Read

🎧 **READ** 25:1 – 26:32

It is a long reading. Summarise what happens. Focus on Paul's speech.

Understand

🎧 **READ** 25:1-12

Verse 6: "Convened" – called together.

- How do the Jews in Jerusalem respond to Festus?
- What do the Jews plan to do?

Festus is the new governor of the province. The Jewish leaders present their charges against Paul again (v2). They ask Festus to bring Paul to Jerusalem—to give them the chance to kill him (v3). But Festus organises a trial in Caesarea.

At the court, the Jews bring serious charges against Paul. But they cannot prove them (v6-7). Paul says he did nothing wrong (v8). This is the same as 24:10-21.

Luke focuses on the attempt to get Paul to travel to Jerusalem (25:9). Paul refuses to go. He says he should be tried by the Romans, not handed over to the Jews (v10-11). Roman citizens were allowed to "appeal to Caesar"—the Roman Emperor (v11). They will be at the highest court in the Roman Empire. Festus agrees Paul can go to Rome (v12). Paul appeals to Caesar to avoid injustice under Festus. He is worried Festus will do something to please the Jews.

🎧 **READ** 25:13-22

- What extra details does Festus give here?
- Why does Luke include this?

King Agrippa was a Jewish king. Festus tells him about Paul. Festus says the main accusation was about religion and Jesus (v18-19). This tells us the real issue: it is not about whether Paul did anything illegal. There is no evidence that he has. The real issue is if Jesus is the Messiah (Christ).

READ 25:23 – 26:23

25:23: "Great pomp" – much ceremony.

26:8: "Incredible" – not possible.

26:14: "Goads" – pointed sticks used to move animals.

- What does Festus want (25:23-27)?
- What does Paul make clear in his speech (26:2-23)?
- What does Paul say is the real reason he is being persecuted?

This is a very impressive occasion with lots of important people (25:23). Festus sums up the situation (v24-27). The important points are: (1) The Jews say Paul should die; (2) Festus finds him innocent; (3) Paul has appealed to Caesar. The question is what charge to write as Paul goes to Rome (v26-27). He hopes Agrippa can help in this.

As a Jew, Agrippa knows the Jewish "customs and controversies"—differences (26:3). So Paul gives a more detailed defence including more religious background. Paul begins with his Jewish background (v4-5). He summarises the main

issue: the hope of the resurrection (v6-8).

These two points summarise his whole speech: (1) the true Jewish hope has been fulfilled; and (2) that is why the Jews are against him.

Paul tells his story. He opposed Jesus. He persecuted believers and travelled around to find more (v9-11). Jesus confronted Paul (v12-18). Jesus questioned Paul's persecution, and said it was persecuting Jesus (v14). "It is hard for you to kick against the goads" means Paul was going against Jesus. Jesus will make sure Paul changes direction.

Paul was appointed as a "witness" of Jesus (v16). Paul was sent to the Jews and the Gentiles (v17). Notice the purpose of this (v18). He would (1) open their eyes, (2) turn them from darkness to light, (3) turn them from the power of Satan to God, (4) which would result in forgiveness of sins, and (5) a place in God's people. This is what happens whenever people believe the good news!

Paul explains what he did then (v19-23). He preached about Jesus and called people to repent. This is why the Jews tried to kill him (v21). Paul shows his message is the message of the Old Testament (v22-23).

40

READ 26:24-32

Verse 28: "Persuade" – convince, make him believe.

- How does Festus respond to Paul?
- How does Paul respond to Festus?
- What appeal does Paul make to Agrippa?

Festus says Paul is "insane" (mad). Festus thinks the story of how Jesus rose from the dead is unbelievable. But Paul says he is not mad and his message is "true and reasonable" (v25). Paul appeals to Agrippa. He says Agrippa knows about these things. They did not happen in secret and so Agrippa must have heard about them. He knows Agrippa believes the prophets in the Old Testament. Paul calls Agrippa to see the truth of what he says.

Paul wants to persuade Agrippa to become a "Christian"—someone who believes in Jesus (v28). Paul prays everyone listening may become a Christian (v29).

Agrippa says Paul could have been set free if he had not appealed to Caesar. We are not to see this as bad, but as God's plan at work.

Find the main point of the passage

- What are the main themes?

- What is different from the earlier trials?

The other trials focused on defending against accusation. This time, Paul wants to persuade his listeners to trust in Jesus. Paul says Jesus fulfils the Old Testament promises. Jesus brings about all of God's plans. Jesus is the way to be saved. Paul wants his listeners to believe the message about Jesus is true.

So the main point is: Paul tries to persuade people to believe in Jesus.

 **PLAN**

Main point of the sermon

Remember, your sermon explains the passage, and applies the passage to your hearers.

Write your main point.

It may be: We must try to persuade people of the message about Jesus.

Sub-points

- Read the main point again.
- Read the verses again.
- What sub-points will help you teach this passage?

The first part (chapter 25) sets the scene. It is chapter 26 we will focus on. Paul makes several key points about Jesus. These can form the sub-points of the sermon.

The sub-points can be:

1. Jesus fulfils God's promises (26:1-8)

2. Jesus brings God's rescue (26:9-23)

3. Everyone should believe in Jesus! (26:24-32)

Illustrate

The main point is about persuading people—helping them to believe something different. Can you think of an example where you tried to persuade people of something? Or someone tried to persuade you? You explained and gave the background. You gave the evidence. You gave personal testimony. Finally, you asked the person to agree. All these are in Paul's speech. He wants to persuade people to believe in Jesus.

Apply

Paul talks about why people should believe in Jesus. It shows us that we should explain to people why and how to trust in Jesus.

This will apply differently in different places. In some countries, people expect us to try to persuade them to believe in Jesus. In other countries, we are not allowed to do that. Encourage people to follow Paul's example and take every opportunity God gives. We must be confident in the message about Jesus. It is a message for everyone—kings and village people. It brings hope and peace with God. Everyone needs to hear the message and be persuaded to believe.

Review

Check the main point is clear and that you keep to THIS passage.

 TEACH

Start

Remind your hearers of some of the background to this passage. This trial and speech are different. Paul tries to persuade people to believe in Jesus. *What will that mean in your situation? What does your government say about talking to others about Jesus? How do believers feel about trying to persuade others? Are they bold or worried? Use your illustration.*

Explain

Summarise the story of chapter 25. Explain what happens between Festus, the Jews and Paul in 25:1-12.

Explain the discussion between Festus and Agrippa in 25:13-22. The Jews want Paul to be killed. Their accusations are really about Jesus and whether he is alive.

The trial starts in 25:23-27. *Explain the points Festus makes.* Paul did nothing that deserved death (v25). So Festus does not know what to write. This gives Paul the opportunity to explain what the main issues are. Paul makes three key points about Jesus.

1. Jesus fulfils God's promises (26:1-8)

Paul points out his Jewish background (v4-5). *Now explain verse 6.* Paul has changed. The hope God promised in the Old Testament is fulfilled in Jesus. This is what Paul now believes. *Show how Paul explains more in verses 7-8.* "It is because of this hope" that Paul is accused. What is this hope? It is the resurrection of the dead, which started in Jesus.

Paul was a faithful Jew, but now he believes this "hope" has come true in Jesus. Jesus fulfils God's promises. So Paul is now a Christian—a Christ follower.

2. Jesus brings God's rescue (26:9-23)

Talk through verses 9-11. Paul was convinced he should oppose Jesus. He thought what believers said about Jesus was wrong and harmful. He was "obsessed"—it was all he could think about (v11). He travelled to foreign cities to find believers (v11).

Tell your people how Paul met with Jesus (v 12-15). Jesus confronted Paul and asked why he was persecuting him. This showed Paul that Jesus is alive. That means Jesus must be the Messiah (Christ). What the Christians said was true.

Explain Jesus' words to Paul in verses 16-18. Jesus chose Paul to explain the message of how to be saved. Paul will explain the message about Jesus. Jesus will:

- open eyes and turn people from darkness to light

- turn people from the power of Satan to God
- bring forgiveness of sins
- join them with God's people who are made holy by faith in Jesus.

Show your hearers what a wonderful message this is!

Jesus said this change comes through "faith in [him]" (v18). *Encourage anyone who has not put their faith in Jesus to do so now.*

Explain the rest of Paul's speech. He preached the message of Jesus to Jews and Gentiles (non-Jews). This was why he was taken hold of by the Jews (v21). They hate what he says about Jesus. But God protected him.

Paul sums up in verses 22-23. He only teaches what the prophets predicted: The Messiah would suffer and then rise from the dead, and the message of Jesus would go to Jews and Gentiles (v22-23).

3. Everyone should believe in Jesus! (26:24-32)

Festus thinks Paul is insane (mad). Paul says he is not insane. What he says is true and reasonable. These events can be proved. *Show how Paul challenges King Agrippa (v27).* Agrippa thinks Paul is trying to persuade him to become a "Christian"—someone who believes this message about Jesus and is saved.

Paul says he prays everyone listening will believe and be saved as he is (v29). Paul wants to persuade everyone to believe.

Apply

We want to persuade people to believe in Jesus. That means we must explain who Jesus is and what he has done. For the Jews, Paul used the Old Testament background. It may be different for people we speak to. But we still want to explain how God has taken action through Jesus. Think how best to do this. We can also use our own story.

Challenge people to respond. Pray about your message, as God's Spirit is needed to open people's eyes.

End

Jesus fulfils all that God promised and what the Old Testament pointed forward to. Jesus is the only way sinners can be put right with a holy God. We want to persuade everyone to believe in Jesus.

Pray

Pray for opportunities to speak about Jesus and persuade people about him.

41 ⬆ STUDY YOU CANNOT STOP GOD

Background

In Paul's journey to Jerusalem and Caesarea, we have seen God rescue him from many dangerous situations. Jesus assured Paul that he will witness about him in Rome (see 23:11). This passage shows God's protection so that Paul will arrive in Rome. This passage is long, but it is one story.

Read

READ 27:1 – 28:16 out loud.

Follow Paul's journey on the map as you read. Summarise the whole story in your own words.

Understand

READ 27:1-12

- What do you notice about this journey?

Notice Luke says "we" in verse 1. He has joined Paul and travels to Rome with him. Rome is to the west. The first trouble comes in verse 4. The ship is forced to go north, to the east of Cyprus. This protects them from the wind. Ships were moved only by the wind blowing their sails.

The real problems start in verse 7. They make slow progress and cannot land at Cnidus. So they sail to the east side of Crete and land

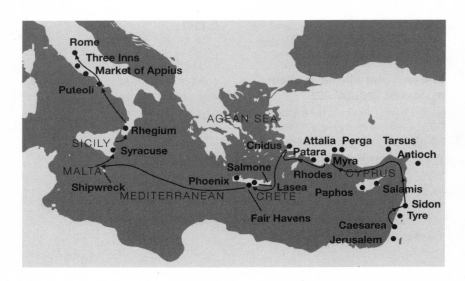

at "Fair Havens". It was "after the Day of Atonement" (the end of September). Sailing became very dangerous at this time of year because of bad weather (v9). Paul advises stopping the journey (v10). But the Roman soldier decides to spend the winter in a better harbour (v12).

READ 27:13-26

- What happens in verses 13-20?
- What important points does Paul make in verses 21-26?

They try to sail west round the island of Crete (v13). But a very strong wind starts (v14). They give up trying to sail where they want, and are carried along by the wind (v15). The lifeboat was usually pulled behind the ship. The storm was so bad the lifeboat is in danger of being blown away (v16-17).

The men pass ropes round the ship to hold it together (v17). They throw the cargo and ship's equipment overboard (v18-19). After many days of stormy weather, they give up all hope (v20).

Then Paul speaks. An angel assured Paul of God's plan for him to witness before Caesar. Remember Jesus' words in 23:11. So Paul must be saved and not drown. God will also

kindly save the lives of everyone else. They will run aground on an island (27:26).

READ 27:27-44

Verse 33: "Constant suspense"— worried all the time

- What happens in verses 27-32?
- What comfort does Paul give in verses 33-38?
- How do we feel when we finally read verse 44?

The sailors realise they are close to land. They worry they will be thrown against rocks. So they put anchors down (v28-29). They pretend to lower more anchors while trying to escape (v30). Paul sees and tells the Roman soldier. Everyone must stay with the ship (v31).

Paul speaks to everyone again. He assures them that no one will be hurt (v34). They should eat something (v33-34). Notice Paul trusts in God's protection and also takes practical steps.

They try to run the ship into a sandy beach but fail. The ship starts to break up (v41). The soldiers plan to kill the prisoners. If a prisoner escaped, the soldiers would be responsible. But the centurion protects them all. Everyone swims

41

or holds onto pieces of wood. Everyone reaches the shore safely.

Notice that God protects them and keeps his promise. So much went wrong, and there were many threats to their lives, but God kept them safe.

READ 28:1-16

- How do we feel when we hear about the snake biting Paul?
- How does God care for the ship's crew and passengers on the island?

On the island of Malta, they are cared for by the local people. As Paul collects wood, he is bitten by a poisonous snake. Another problem for Paul! The islanders think Paul must be a murderer and that the gods are punishing him. When the snake does not hurt Paul, they think he is a god! This is not true. It is God protecting Paul again.

God then allows Paul to heal people. The islanders honour them in many ways. When they leave, the islanders give them the supplies they need. So, after a terrible time and much danger, they are cared for.

The rest of the journey to Rome has no problems (v11-14). As Paul comes close to Rome, believers come to meet him. Paul is encouraged (v15). In Rome, Paul lives in a house rather than in prison, but a solider guards him.

Find the main point of the passage

- Why does Luke give so much information about this journey?
- What point is Luke making?

Luke gives the details so we see how dangerous the journey was. There were many threats to Paul's life. But he arrives in Rome safely. We see that his safe arrival is a miracle. God had said that Paul would go to Rome to testify about Christ. God keeps that promise, whatever the opposition.

This is one message of Acts. The message about Jesus will keep spreading across the world. God is at work and nothing can stop him.

So the main point is: God's plan for the spread of the message about Jesus cannot be stopped.

 **PLAN**

Main point of the sermon

Write your main point.

Your main point may be: It is God who is spreading the good news about Jesus and so nothing will stop it.

Sub-points

- Read the main point again.
- Read the verses again.
- What sub-points will help you teach this passage?

The main point is that nothing can stop God's plans. Opposition can never stop God. But this does not mean God's people do nothing. Paul is active in practical ways. God's people are active to help him.

The sub points can be:

1. Nothing can stop God's plans

2. We must be active

3. We must help each other

This is one story with three points, so there are no verses given for each part.

Illustrate

On the Apollo 13 space mission to the moon, many things went wrong. An explosion damaged the space ship. Then different problems threatened the lives of the crew. It looked like they would die. It looked like a disaster. But then someone said: "This is going to be our finest hour". Their greatness was seen in coming through all the problems.

It is like that in this passage. We do not see God's power by Paul having an easy journey. We see God's power to bring Paul through everything that goes wrong.

Apply

This passage teaches us that God's plans will win whatever opposition comes. That gives us confidence in God and his plans. This passage shows God will make sure his message goes out. That is what Jesus said will happen (Acts 1:8). It gives us confidence to spread the message about Jesus with courage.

God's power is not seen in him preventing opposition. God's power is seen in bringing us through opposition. We need to be active and involved, but trust that God will bring about his plans. We need to help each other in this great work.

Review

Check the main point is clear and that you keep to THIS passage.

TEACH

Start

How do your hearers feel when the message of Jesus is opposed? We may feel afraid and want to give up. This passage encourages us to press on and trust God, whatever opposition comes. *Use your illustration.* Sometimes power is only seen by getting through difficulties.

Remind people what has happened. Paul witnessed to the good news about Jesus in Jerusalem. God said he would testify in Rome. Paul's life was in danger many times, but God defended and protected Paul.

Explain

It is best to explain the whole story and then bring out the lessons for us.

Tell the story

Talk through the whole passage. Use the notes in the STUDY pages to help. Point out all the times something goes wrong. This includes:

- *what happens with the weather (27:7-8, 14-15, 18)*
- *the decisions the captain takes (27:11)*
- *the sailors trying to escape (27:30)*
- *the ship starting to break up (27:41)*
- *the soldiers planning to kill the prisoners (27:42)*

- *Paul being bitten by a poisonous snake (28:3)*

Point out how hopeless everyone feels (27:20, 29). Help your hearers to understand some of the details and see how it did not seem possible for Paul to reach Rome alive. Then explain what we can learn from the passage.

1. Nothing can stop God's plans

Read 23:11. Now Paul travels to Rome and everything goes wrong. Paul's life is in danger many times from different reasons. This is Satan trying to stop Paul getting to Rome.

Show it is a miracle that Paul arrived at Rome! This shows it was God at work. God has a plan for Paul and nothing can stop it. Jesus said his followers will be his witnesses in Jerusalem, Judea and Samaria, and to the ends of the earth (1:8). We have followed each part of that through Acts. This gives us confidence that God will make sure his message spreads over the whole earth.

Encourage people with how the good news about Jesus is spreading in many parts of the world today. God has a plan and nothing will stop him.

2. We must be active

Nothing will stop God. But we have a part to do. We must not think:

God is doing all the work so we can do nothing. In this passage God is at work, but Paul is still very active. *Show examples such as 27:33-36.* Paul tells people they will be saved. But he also says they must eat. They are weak and need strength to swim. God's promise of rescue does not mean they sit and wait.

This is how God usually works. We must trust his sovereign rule (his complete control) over us, and we must get on with what he wants us to do. We must make decisions and be responsible.

3. We must help each other

We see how Paul was encouraged on his journey by God's people. *Point out the following verses:*

- *27:3: Friends of Paul provide for his needs.*
- *28:14: Believers in Puteoli invite Paul and the others to stay with them.*
- *28:15: Believers from Rome come to meet Paul.*

Point out Paul's reaction in the last example. Believers come from Rome to meet him and walk with him into the city. Paul is encouraged because they show care for him. So, in this terrible journey, God's people care for Paul.

Apply

Remind your hearers that God's plans can never be stopped. God said the message about Jesus will spread everywhere, and it will. God's kingdom will never stop growing. That gives us confidence to spread the message about Jesus, whatever difficulties we face. It will not be easy. But God's power is seen as his people continue, however hard it is.

Encourage people that trusting God's plans goes with being active. We should make plans and be responsible. But as we do so, we trust God's control over all things.

Challenge people to care for and help one another. We need each other as we press on through difficult times.

End

Nothing can stop God. We can confidently press on spreading the message about Jesus.

Pray

Pray your church will know this confidence in God. Pray you will know God's help and protection when difficulties come. Pray you will press on and help each other.

42 ⬆ STUDY
SADNESS AND VICTORY

Background

This is the last passage in the book of Acts. Some of the main themes are summarised. We especially see the reaction of the Jews to the message about Jesus.

Read

READ 28:17-31 two or three times.

Write each verse in your own words.

Understand

READ verses 17-22

Verse 22: "Sect" – a religious group, often within a larger religion.

- Why does Paul call the leaders of the Jews so that he can speak to them?
- What does he tell them?
- How do they respond?

Paul speaks to the Jewish leaders. He wants to clear up any wrong understanding. Also, Paul always goes first to the Jews to tell them about Jesus, as they are God's people. Paul tells them what happened in Jerusalem and defends his actions.

Paul wants to tell them about "the hope of Israel" (v20). This is that Jesus fulfilled the promises of the Old Testament through his death and resurrection (rising to life). It is because of this hope that Paul is in chains (v20).

The Jews in Rome want to hear from Paul, because people everywhere talk against this sect (v22).

READ verses 23-31

- What does Paul speak about to the Jews?
- How does this repeat main themes from the book of Acts?
- What is the reaction to the message about Jesus (v24)?
- How does Paul explain this reaction in verses 25-28?
- Does the book end in a positive or negative way?

Paul teaches the Jews about the "kingdom of God"—how God started his rule through Jesus. Paul tries to convince them about Jesus from the Old Testament (v23). Paul did this in all his journeys.

The reaction is mixed. We saw this before. Some believe in Christ, but some do not believe. Paul explains this reaction with words from Isaiah 6:9-10. Jesus also quotes these words about people's response to him (Mark 4:10-12; and see John 12:37-41). Isaiah's words tell of people who hear but will not understand. This is because their hearts are "calloused" (hard).

Rejection by the Jews means the message of salvation will go to the Gentiles (Acts 28:28). We have seen this before. God always planned for the Gentiles to hear the message about Jesus after the Jews (see Romans 1:16).

The book ends with sadness and victory. There is sadness over so many Jews rejecting the good news. God's people should welcome his message but many reject it. There is victory because the message is spreading among the Gentiles.

Paul can speak the message with "boldness"—confidence. And he speaks "without hindrance". Paul is kept inside his house, but there are no barriers to the message about Jesus spreading.

We are not told what happens to Paul. Luke wants to show that the unstoppable message of Jesus continues to go out to more and more people. Jesus said his disciples would be his witnesses across the world (1:8). That is what we have seen happen. Praise God!

Find the main point of the passage

- Why does Luke finish his book in this way?
- What is the main feeling we have as the book closes?
- What themes from earlier in Acts are repeated here?

The book finishes by proclaiming the good news about Jesus. Paul tries to persuade a group of Jews.

Some believe, but many reject the good news. There is a feeling of deep sadness. This is God's message for them but they will not believe.

But Paul is confident the Gentiles "will listen" (28:28). So the book finishes with Paul teaching about the kingdom of God and the Lord Jesus. It finishes on a note of victory.

The passage summarises the message of Acts. The message about Jesus will be rejected by some but it will continue to spread.

PLAN

Main point of the sermon

Write your main point.

The main theme is that many people reject God's message, but God's message still goes forward.

Sub-points

- Read the main point again.
- Read the verses again.
- What sub-points will help you teach this passage?

The sub points may be:

1. Be sad when God's message is rejected (v17-27)

2. Be confident of God's message spreading (v28-31)

Illustrate

Imagine you promise to buy a special gift for someone. You tell them it is coming. It is just right for them. They should receive it with joy and thanks. But they reject it. That is how many Jews respond to Paul's message. The good news of Jesus is about how God kept his promises to his people. Jesus is the "hope of Israel" (v20). But many Jews reject God's gift. That is very sad.

But others will gladly receive that gift. The Gentiles receive the forgiveness of sins that God offers in Jesus.

Apply

There is a specific application to Jews who will not believe the good news about Jesus. They should receive the message as God's promises coming true. But it is sad when anyone rejects the good news of forgiveness. It shows their hearts are hard. We are not surprised when that happens, but we are sad. Ask your hearers if they have believed or rejected God's message. Encourage any who are not believers to ask God to open their ears and eyes that they too may believe.

We must be confident of the victory of the good news. Jesus said the message about him would spread across the world: That is what happens in Acts and is continuing to happen now. The kingdom of God is growing bigger and bigger as more and more people believe. The book of Acts finishes with the victory of the message about Jesus.

Review

Check the main point is clear and you keep to THIS passage.

 **TEACH**

Start

Acts began with Jesus talking about the spread of his message (1:8). We have seen this happen. Now the message is in Rome—the centre of the Roman Empire. The spread of the gospel causes us mixed feelings.

Explain

1. Be sad when God's message is rejected (v17-27)

Explain Paul's meeting with Jews in Rome. Paul defends himself and the message about Jesus. The Jews want to hear from him. Paul explains how God brings his rule over the world (v23). God does that through Jesus. Paul tries to convince the Jews from the Old Testament. Paul has done this throughout Acts.

Some Jews believe, but others refuse to believe. We saw this before. Isaiah 6:9-10 explains how Jews respond to Isaiah's message. They do not believe because of their hard hearts. This is very sad. These people should accept what Paul said, but they turn away from God.

This is particularly true of Jews, but is also true of anyone who rejects the message about Jesus. God offers them forgiveness through Jesus, but they reject it. This is sad.

2. Be confident of God's message spreading (v28-31)

Explain verse 28. Paul does not mean every Gentile will listen. But there will be a better response. We have seen this in Acts. Paul spoke to Gentiles and many believed.

Explain Paul's ministry (v 30-31). Paul teaches about the kingdom of God and Jesus. Paul speaks "with boldness" and with no limits. Paul is guarded in his house, but nothing stops the message of how to be saved through Jesus from going out.

Jesus' words in Acts 1:8 come true throughout Acts and in this passage. *Use your illustration.* We feel sad when people reject the message about Jesus. But we are confident it will continue spreading.

Apply

Some people reject the good news of Jesus. We are sad for them. But we are confident God's message will spread. The book of Acts finishes on that note of victory. God's kingdom will grow. That encourages us to keep spreading God's message.

End

Sadly, some will reject the good news. But we are confident in God and his plans.

Pray

Pray for greater confidence in God and for the growth of his kingdom.

PPP ALSO AVAILABLE

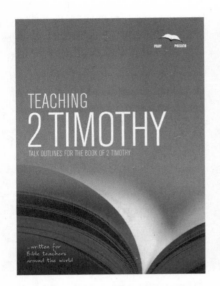

TEACHING
2 TIMOTHY
TALK OUTLINES FOR THE BOOK OF 2 TIMOTHY

...written for
Bible teachers
around the world

TEACHING
DEUTERONOMY
TALK OUTLINES FOR THE BOOK OF DEUTERONOMY

...written for
Bible teachers
around the world

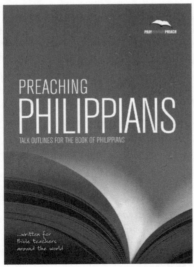

PREACHING
PHILIPPIANS
TALK OUTLINES FOR THE BOOK OF PHILIPPIANS

...written for
Bible teachers
around the world

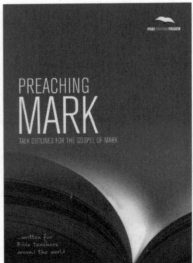

PREACHING
MARK
TALK OUTLINES FOR THE GOSPEL OF MARK

...written for
Bible teachers
around the world

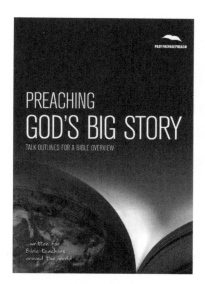

God's Big Story provides pastors and teachers with a series of studies focusing on the whole Bible story of salvation.

PPP Teaching the Bible takes people through the stages needed to understand a Bible passage, prepare a talk or sermon, and teach it effectively in a local context.

WWW.THEGOODBOOK.CO.UK/PPP

 **ALSO AVAILABLE**

There is an exciting and growing programme of PPP **translations** that includes Spanish, Hindi, Burmese, Serbian, Khmer, Nepali and French.

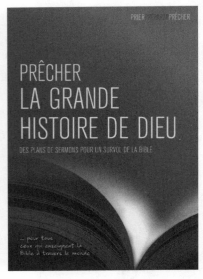

thegoodbook
COMPANY
Opening up the Bible

At The Good Book Company, we are dedicated to helping people understand what Christianity is, and to helping Christians and local churches grow. We believe that God's growth process always starts with hearing clearly what he has said to us through his timeless word—the Bible.

Ever since we opened our doors in 1991, we have been striving to produce resources that honour God in the way the Bible is used. We have grown to become an international provider of user-friendly resources, with people of all backgrounds and denominations using our books, courses and DVDs.

We want to enable people to understand who Jesus is; and to equip ordinary Christians to live for him day by day, and churches to grow in their knowledge of God and in their love for one another and their neighbours.

Call us for a discussion of your needs or visit one of our local websites for more information on the resources and services we provide.

UK & Europe: www.thegoodbook.co.uk
North America: www.thegoodbook.com
Australia: www.thegoodbook.com.au
New Zealand: www.thegoodbook.co.nz

UK & Europe: 0333 123 0880
North America: 866 244 2165
Australia: (02) 6100 4211
New Zealand (+64) 3 343 2463

www.christianityexplored.org
Our partner site is a great place for those exploring the Christian faith, with a clear explanation of the good news, powerful testimonies and answers to difficult questions.

One life. What's it all about?